Along Bible Paths
Summer Devotions

Henry and Jody Neufeld

Energion Publications

P. O. Box 841

Gonzalez, FL 32560

www.energionpubs.com

Energion Publications

P. O. Box 841

Gonzalez, FL 32560

ISBN10: 1-893729-83-4
ISBN13: 978-1-893729-83-4
Library of Congress Control Number: 2010929365

Dedication

To all the generations of our family

FORWARD

May God the Father of our Lord Jesus Christ be blessed. According to his abundant mercy he has given birth to us anew into a living hope through the resurrection of Jesus Christ from the dead, into an incorruptible, undefiled, and unfading inheritance kept in heaven for you. We are guarded by God's power through faith for the salvation which is ready to be revealed in the last time.
6You rejoice in this, though right now it's necessary that you be distressed by many trials,7 so that the quality of your faith might be like preciious gold, refined through fire and proven, and might be found to result in praise, glory, and honor when Jesus Christ is revealed. You love him even though you have not seen him. You have put your confidence in him, even though you can't see him now. You rejoice with an unspeakable and honorable joy,9 receiving the goal of your faith, the salvation of your souls.

1 Peter 1:3-9

Today, more than ever, most of us need help navigating through each day with its uncertainties, stress, and responsibilities. The number of self-help books and publications produced to give the reader some sense of control and insight into their future decisions and subsequent consequences is staggering. Who has answers? What can be believed?

For the mountains may go away and the hills fall,
but my gracious mercy to you will not go away
and the peace agreement I have given you will not fall,
says Yahweh who has compassion on you.

Isaiah 54:10

Henry and I bring together the tradition of "I the Lord do not change" (Malachi 3:6) and "See, I am doing a new thing" (Isaiah 43:19) in the way we pursue our personal Bible study. I am always learning something new when Henry shares Biblical history and language nuances. I am always looking at how a passage applies to my life now, soaking up the timeless application of God's Word. As you are searching for directions to the answers of your life's questions, pray that you will find that it is in building your relationship with God that you live in peace and joy that is not dependent upon circumstances. If you come near to God with study of His Word and open conversation with Him, He will be found near to you. Come on in!

– Jody Neufeld

"This is my commandment, that you love one another, even as I have loved you. Greater love has no one than this, that someone lay down his life for his friends. You are my friends, if you do whatever I command you. No longer do I call you servants, for the servant doesn't know what his lord does. But I have called you friends, *for everything that I heard from my Father, I have made known to you."*

John 15:12-15 (WEB, my emphasis)

It is a wonderful (that word does not really express my heart but I'll use it) – a wonderful place in my life that I **know** that I am **God's friend** and **He is my friend!** For many years, our relationship would have been described as **acquaintances.** Friendship means both parties not only want to be friends but are willing to put forth the effort it takes to make and keep the friendship. God's effort was done when Jesus made the perfect sacrifice that covered all my sins. My effort is a daily choice to be His friend and live with Him as He lives with me. It is a life that is marked with **hope, forgiveness, and love.**

Do you know someone who speaks about or lives their life in hope**less**ness? Do they say they do not know how to forgive someone who has hurt or wronged them terribly? Maybe they do not know how to forgive themselves? Do you know someone who is desperately looking for love? Have you offered them Jesus? How long are **we** going to allow them to suffer?

There are as many ways to show Jesus to someone as there are – commercials for cell phones! I just have to be willing **and** loving!

Live my life as Jesus' ambassador. Walk out my life in the **spirit** and **truth** of who Jesus is. That means that anyone who meets me – meets Jesus' kindness, gentleness, compassion, and forgiveness. I am what I show myself to be. Not perfect – just forgiven! This is the primary way to share Jesus with the world and we have no excuse not to do it! However, I do not believe it is the only way. People are going to ask, "How do you survive _____?" or "You never seem to get frustrated in this job. How do you do that?" A shrug or suggestion to take up palates is taking the easy way out and avoiding giving God the first credit for your life!

Share briefly how God has changed how you live or think. Everyone should have a three point, brief story to share about 1) how I was, 2) what happened/when I decided to make a change, and 3) how Jesus helped me to where I am now. It is not a sermon. It is a brief way to share that Jesus and your relationship with Him has made the difference that they see. You are not convincing them – you are sharing Who has changed you!

Suggest they might want to listen or read something about Jesus that has helped you. Maybe you have recently read a Max Lucado book or listened to a CD that you could suggest. I have discovered a website that is **awesome** for someone who maybe **did** know Jesus but has let their relationship slide away or they think Jesus could not possibly forgive them for what they have done. It is www.prodigalsonly.com. It is Jesus in the 21st century – inviting the prodigal home!

"I call you friends..." Come meet my best friend, Jesus. You'll like Him.

Take a Step
July 2

For to this you were called, because Christ also suffered for us, leaving you an example, that you should follow his steps,...
1 Peter 2:21 (WEB)

I have been thinking about how Jesus leads me **a step** at a time. He shows me or shows my husband a vision of the goal or mission but He does not give us the whole plan. He does not give me, personally more than one step at a time. If Jesus is giving Henry more than one step, He is also telling him to keep them under wraps!

I believe Jesus only gives me one step because He knows me. He knows that if He gave me several steps I would try to **tweak** them – just to give it a little more efficiency or improve it a bit! SO – Jesus wisely tells me only one step!

Since I only know one step, Jesus is building my trust level, isn't He? I do not know what is around the bend on this journey I am on so I trust Jesus to bring me through whatever mountain or moat I am about to encounter. I know that nothing takes Him by surprise so Jesus knows the route I need to take through this obstacle. I may not know all these events but I **do know** how the story is going to end.

The one step journey also increases my prayer life as I want to build my spiritual muscles for the journey at hand. Any concerns (that's another word for **worry**), questions, even fears, I take to Jesus to sift through the emotions and bring the truth to my mind. Conversations with Jesus happen at any time, day or night, and bring me to the place where I am **ready** for the next step.

Do I step with joy? Do I step with thanksgiving? Is my step firm or tentative? Do I march like a soldier or do I drag my feet? Ouch.

Your testimonies are wonderful, therefore my soul keeps them.
The entrance of your words gives light. It gives understanding to the simple.
I opened my mouth wide and panted, for I longed for your commandments.
Turn to me, and have mercy on me, as you always do to those

who love your name.
Establish my footsteps in your word. Don't let any iniquity
have dominion over me.

Psalm 119:129-133 (WEB)

Taste and see that God is Good!   July 3

Oh taste and see that Yahweh is good. Blessed is the man who
takes refuge in him.   *Psalm 34:8 (WEB)*

We are coming up on one of my favorite holidays – July 4th! Like most holidays it involves great food and family. What more could you want? **FIREWORKS!!!** I am a watcher of fireworks. I will be checking the TV listings to make sure I watch every firework display that is presented. I like seeing them in person but this year I will be at home watching on TV.

July 4th is a time that we remember the joy and victory of our freedoms. We recite portions of the Declaration of Independence and Constitution like beautiful pieces of poetry. Lincoln's Gettysburg Address and Kennedy's Inaugural Address bring tears to the eyes that only truly inspired works can do. It is a feast for the spirit as we share a gastronomic feast among family and friends.

I hope as we celebrate we also remember our Lord who was there every step of the way. As we celebrate may we also raise our voices in thanksgiving for our Lord who did not leave us on the battlefields nor sleep while we debated and voted our way through presidents, senators, representatives, governors, mayors, and thousands of laws. As we sit around the table and share wonderful memories of picnics passed, may we also share stories of how our Lord fed us when we could not feed ourselves. It is not about preaching or arguing to win a point – it is about telling our story, "Look what the Lord has done!"

Hear my teaching, my people. Turn your ears to the words of my mouth.

I will open my mouth in a parable. I will utter dark sayings of old, which we have heard and known, and our fathers have told us.

We will not hide them from their children, telling to the generation to come the praises of Yahweh, his strength, and his wondrous works that he has done.

For he established a testimony in Jacob, and appointed a teaching in Israel, which he commanded our fathers, that they should make them known to their children; that the generation to come might know, even the children who should be born; who should arise and tell their children, that they might set their hope in God, and not forget the works of God, but keep his commandments, and might not be as their fathers, a stubborn and rebellious generation, a generation that didn't make their hearts loyal, whose spirit was not steadfast with God.

Psalm 78:1-8 (WEB)

On July 4th what will you remember about the holiday? Will you be able to know that you shared a piece of your heart as you told the story of how Jesus helped you through the week? Will you dismiss the question because you did not want to offend someone? Will that hold up as you look at Jesus and explain that the truth is – you were ashamed of Him? Will He be ashamed of you? Will He bless you with the rest of one who has "done well, good and faithful servant!"? I pray that it is so – for you **and** me. God bless America!

Hope   July 4

...And the mystery is that Christ lives in you, and he is your hope of sharing in God's glory.

Colossians 1:27 (CEV)

Why do we say that our hope is in Jesus Christ?

'Hope' is expecting a desire to be fulfilled. If I have 'hope', I am optimistic about my future. Before I accepted my need for a savior and that Jesus is my Savior, I had only what I could see with my eyes. I had only this world and what it could give me. Frankly – if THIS is all that there is – I want a refund on my life!

- Gas prices are climbing – Vacation? Not happening. I want to move closer to my work to save money!
- War in several countries with young men and women making tremendous sacrifices, including their lives.
- Health care costs are climbing and insurance coverage is declining. Even those of us who have insurance have to figure out how to afford the co-pay.
- Violence is no longer something we see in wars and in movies or TV but it is in our workplace, our schools, and on our roads.
- Marriage is considered an 'option' for those in love and children with parents married to each other and leading lives to be imitated are rare.

Hope is what I see when I look at Jesus. Hope is what I know when I read God's truth. Hope is what strengthens me when my world is shook with disease, death, and situations I cannot understand. Hope comes when I go to my knees.

Jesus, God Himself, came to this earth and took on the life that we have here. He walked. He slept on the ground. He was mocked by ignorant people. He put out His hands to help and people wanted to stone Him. He healed ten lepers and only one said, "Thanks". Jesus came to my life, in this world, and walked so that I would have hope when I had to walk the same roads.

Paul speaks of hope to the Romans reminding them that hope is expecting something you cannot see. If you can see it, then you don't hope for it! **And** Jesus knew that we need help to hope and so He sent us His Spirit to strengthen us in our weakness. (Romans 8:18-39) Take a few minutes today and read the passage in Romans. Soak in the words and allow **hope** to grow inside of you.

Trust   July 5

In God, I praise his word. In God, I put my trust.

Psalm 56:4 (WEB)

Do you trust God? With how much do you trust Him? To trust someone is to rely on them with an assurance that comes from what you know about their character, their strength, and their truth. So how much I trust God is directly affected by how much I **know** about God! And it's not a 'theory' of knowing but an actual 'in practice' of knowing!

Did you ever play that game where you are blindfolded and you are to fall backwards into someone's arms? It is a test of trust. Military personnel, law enforcement, and firefighters must form bonds of trust in their company and between partners. They must know that when they go through the door or down an alley, the one next to them or behind them will be well-trained and willing to give all they have to protect them.

Going through life with Jesus is like that. I need a bond with Him. I have learned that going through a crisis situation with the assurance that He is with me is so much better than going through a crisis looking for some assurance.

I am sure you can think of many who seem to walk with such trust in God. But most of them did not **start** at trust. They had to work their way **up** to trust!

Esther – Most known for her heroic saving of her people by being obedient to be used "for a time such as this". (Esther

4:14) Esther was snatched into captivity and was counseled and encouraged by her uncle, Mordecai, to respond with such boldness to the king, her husband, who had the power to kill her.

Joshua – Joshua is told over and over by God to "be strong and courageous" and to move on after the death of Moses. He listened to the Lord for himself and learned to hear God's voice and be obedient to His voice. **Then** the walls of Jericho fell down!

Peter – After denying Jesus three times and running away with the rest of the disciples, Peter, the little-educated fisherman, stands up in front of thousands of Jews and gives the first New Testament altar call! He became the Rock that Jesus saw! He trusted God.

Some trust in chariots, and some in horses, but we trust the name of Yahweh our God.

Psalms 20:7 (WEB)

Are you willing to take another step closer to God and another step deeper in trust of God today? Is there something or someone in your life (even yourself!) that you just do not know what to do? Have you been reading self-help books and advice columns, talked to your friends and asked their advice and still are unsure what to do? How is that option working for you? **Give God your trust. He will not let you down!** There is no magic formula. It is just letting go "of the way you've always done it" and letting God do the rest!

Come, Lord Jesus, come! Guide and direct me where You will! I trust you for **all** things and will **not** forget to thank and praise you when it is over.

...My heart and my flesh cry out for the living God.

Psalm:84:2 (WEB)

My week started out thinking about 'flesh' and how it's a battle to direct my flesh in the right path!

God blessed me by reminding me of the step of faith that I took over 10 years ago and how that faith has grown. I also reflected this week on the roots of faith that my mother sewed as she taught me as a young child to pray.

I wept several times this week as I looked at the hope that I have ...that I've been given in Jesus Christ! Yes, I am unworthy! YES, I don't deserve it! But God, my Father, gave His Son so that He could spend eternity with me! WOW!

I went to sleep last night thinking back how Jesus has been growing my trust in Him. He has stayed with me through some rocky paths. He has waited patiently even when I turned away in despair and frustration and, when I turned back around, He was there with open arms. That hug was great!!!

Flesh is about making choices. God offers me so much to fill my mind and heart and spirit. He gives me gifts that multiply fruit, lots and lots of fruit!!! The more I accept and use the gifts – the more the fruit increases!

But the fruit of the Spirit is love, joy, peace, patience, kindness, goodness, faith, gentleness, and self-control.
Galatians 5:22-23 (WEB)

Finally, brothers, whatever things are true, whatever things are honorable, whatever things are just, whatever things are pure, whatever things are lovely, whatever things are of good report; if there is any virtue, and if there is any praise, think about these things.

Philippians 4:8 (WEB)

Enough said! However, this is what I have learned this week: Whenever I allow my flesh to drag me down and focus on the world and its sorrows and 'no answers' or 'poor answers', if I will then pick my head up and look at **Jesus,** I have taken a step forward! Pull out God's Word and **stop** to tune in to God's voice, the voice of **truth! Choose God!** My next thought, my next step then comes along side of God. Then I stay on God's true path. That is where I want to be!

Let us thank our Lord today for this great country He has blessed and continues to bless. May we turn more to Him as a nation. May we glorify Him as we reach out to others and come together in unity! Let us lift up our men and women in uniform both in the armed forces here and over seas and those who protect us across our country as police officers and fire fighters. God bless them every one! In Jesus' name I pray...Amen.

Intercessory Prayer   July 7

> *"I pray for them. I don't pray for the world, but for those whom you have given me, for they are yours."*
>
> *John 17:9 (WEB)*

I have had two conversations recently that has given me some new perspective to intercessory prayer.

Bringing someone to the Lord in prayer is **intercessory prayer.** To be honest, I always thought that intercessory prayer was about **me** pointing out something that **God** had overlooked in someone and then attempt to talk **Him** into **my** idea! Crazy, huh?

Reading through John 17 I am **struck** by the love and compassion of Jesus. **That** is intercessory prayer! It is allowing God to give me **His** vision for that person. It is allowing God to change my heart for His heart and pray for the person in Jesus' love. Bringing someone into God's presence changes **my** attitude toward them. It will affect my relationship with them. I am changed into seeing that person as God sees them. I also learn how God sees **me.** I see the unique gifts and unique flaws that ultimately create the tapestry that is in God's image.

There are principles of God that I know to be true as I pray. I know that God desires a living, growing, intimate relationship with each of His children. I know that He wants His children to be spiritually strong to resist temptation and not be lead into evil. God wants His children to reach out to others and serve them.

Praying for others also gives me a glimpse into how God must feel as He looks at us and wants so much 'good' for us and yet does not impose His will into our lives. Our God who **could**, chooses instead to honor our freedom to choose. And as I pray I see changes that may need to happen. But as most parents realize their limitations in coercing a child into a path, so in prayer I learn to pray and let go, trusting the Holy Spirit to lead the person in God's perfect path.

Every intercessory prayer begins with God who was there in the situation before I even knew there was a situation! Every intercessory prayer ends with God who never tires or grows weary (Isaiah 40:28-31) and will see the person and/or situation until the end. As my husband, Henry, says:

"God answers our prayers better than we pray them!"

God will answer in His time and in His perfect way. It is a joy to pray no matter what the circumstances when I pray in the assurance of God's love and mercy.

"I am the first, and I am the last; and besides me there is no God.
Who is like me? Who will call, and will declare it, and set it in order for me, since I established the ancient people?
Let them declare the things that are coming, and that will happen.
Don't fear, neither be afraid.
Haven't I declared it to you long ago, and shown it?

11

You are my witnesses. Is there a God besides me?
Indeed, there is not. I don't know any other Rock."

Isaiah 44:6-8 (WEB)

As we come to the Lord in prayer, may we always have our feet on the Rock and cry out to our God, who is the First and the Last. Amen.

Waiting Eagerly and Patiently   July 8

But if we hope for what we do not see, we wait for it patiently.

Romans 8:25 (HN)

"Wait" is a four letter word. The way most of us think of it (and I'm included here) we could use it to cuss someone out. In modern American culture, we do not like to wait. Think about that as you read this devotional, which I'm going to present more or less as it happened to me.

One day Jody told me that she wouldn't get a devotional done. For various reasons it had simply fallen off the priority list. I said I'd try to get one out.

In the morning I started to look at lectionary texts. Part of my personal devotionals is to take a daily look at current lectionary readings. I've been amazed at what God led me to. For unknown reasons (you may surmise what you wish) I started my reading with the verse that is coming up in two weeks, Romans 8:12-25. I normally start with the Old Testament reading, then read the Psalm, then the gospel, and finally the epistle. But I started with Paul this time.

I ended up focusing my thoughts on verse 25 which I have quoted above, using my own draft translation. There's something I want to look into later in that verse, because the word used for "wait" there often includes the idea of waiting expectantly or eagerly. Paul adds the word "patiently." At this point I was distracted from my reading and left the rest of my reading for later in the day. I had to drive Jody to work at 7 am, one of the reasons she's was not writing the devotional.

I was combining meditation on the combination of "eagerness" and "patience" and at the same time wondering whether that aspect of the word should be translated in this verse (most English translations do not). So I was switching between thinking about the technical aspects of the passage and the spiritual idea of combining patience with eagerness.

I left Jody at work and went on toward a gas station. I had let the tank run very low, but thought I would reach the station comfortably. It was not to be. Probably a half mile from the nice discount station I intended to use, the car sputtered a few times and then stopped permanently. The positive side of this was that I was near a mall and that I was able to get into the parking lot and sort of sputter into a parking place. I also did not have a gas can, so I had to go in search of a gas station that might also supply a gas can.

Now if you want to test my patience in the most severe way, interfere with my morning. I get up early, usually between 5 and 6 am, and I find that I do my best work before lunch. Oh, I can work after lunch, but I don't accomplish as much per hour.

Patience and eagerness combined. Picture me walking around, getting directions, finding a gas station, buying a gas can and a couple of gallons of gas, then starting to walk back. All of this was accomplished with what seems like remarkable speed looking back, but which I greeted with marked impatience at the time.

As I was walking back, I see some flowers in various beds in front of the mall. I think "Those are really pretty." as I'm walking on by. Suddenly I knew I was supposed to stop and take a picture. Those who know me know that I'm not all that much for taking pictures unless there's a specific purpose, and I'm not very good at it in any case. I could see no particular reason to take a picture of these flowers.

I took a couple more steps and the feeling grew stronger. I needed to stop a take a picture. So using the camera in my little Palm Centro that serves me as a substitute brain, I stopped and took a picture, not of just one flower bed, but four of them. The interesting thing was that as I looked at the flowers, decided how to do the picture, and so forth, I relaxed. I started to enjoy myself.

I was eager to get home and get to work, but patience came to me. I believe that patience was the presence of God in my eagerness. It's not wrong for me to be eager to get to my work and writing, but at the same time, I have to be prepared to take time with God along the way.

We have so many of these combinations in our Christian lives. We are saved by God's grace through no action or merit of our own, yet we are expected to act and live life according to God's will. While we may strive to do God's will, we do not claim to have attained that level of obedience. Jesus came as a human being into this world, according to orthodox theology, both 100% human and 100% divine. That doesn't make a great deal of sense to us by human logic, but we believe it nonetheless. We are to wait for the second coming of Jesus, which is soon, but yet it seems like it will never come.

Often when we try to resolve these things through human logic we wind up heading right into classic heresies. Faith vs. works arguments have led more astray than is easy to count. Waiting for the second coming has tempted many people to provide a date for that event, even though Jesus said it wouldn't work.

For me, this morning, patience and eagerness didn't work together. The idea of waiting both patiently and eagerly was quite illogical. I was ready to believe it, should I conclude that

14

was what God was saying, but I didn't understand it. That is, until God stepped in for a moment in time and shifted my perspective.

I felt God's grace in my life this morning, and the **means** was an empty gas tank, a few flowers, and God's Spirit reaching out to touch me. That's not the usual means of grace, but God often proves he can work through unexpected things.

(You can find the flower pictures from this devotional on the back cover of this book.)

Love   July 9

> *If I speak with the languages of men and of angels, but don't have love, I have become sounding brass, or a clanging cymbal. If I have the gift of prophecy, and know all mysteries and all knowledge; and if I have all faith, so as to remove mountains, but don't have love, I am nothing. If I dole out all my goods to feed the poor, and if I give my body to be burned, but don't have love, it profits me nothing.*
>
> *1 Corinthians 13:1-3 (WEB)*

This is one of those passages (and the rest of the 13th chapter) that is good for me to read in an unfamiliar translation. In the NIV, I have read these verses so many times that I do not take the words in and allow them to saturate me and soak me with their truth and wisdom...with their love.

It is the **love** part that I so often glide through in search of some **meat** when it is **love** that is the **power** and **core** of God Himself! It is love that brought Jesus up from His knees in Gethsemane and set his path unswervingly to Golgotha. It is love that kicks satan and his buddies every time they bring selfishness, bitterness, unforgiveness, and pride and we choose compassion, joy, gentleness, and humility instead.

When was the last time you read 1 Corinthians 13 or Song of Songs? How about John 17 where Jesus **intercedes** for us? It is love that is in every letter and period. From Genesis to Revelation we are shown the many facets of God's love. Even in the discipline and consequences there is love, the perfect love of a Father for His child. And as His disciple, I am to follow this love; be an ambassador of His love. I am not to store that love for some rainy day. I am not to just soak it up and lock it inside myself. It is to **flow** through me, untainted by me. I am just a conduit of God's love to others who do not truly know Him or are too scared to meet Him. It is His unconditional and extravagant love that will 'woo' them to come closer to 'taste and see that God is good'! (Psalm 34:8)

Take time today to soak in God's love. Read the following verses and then go **spill** them on someone!

Love is patient and is kind; love doesn't envy. Love doesn't brag, is not proud, doesn't behave itself inappropriately, doesn't seek its own way, is not provoked, takes no account of evil; doesn't rejoice in unrighteousness, but rejoices with the truth; bears all things, believes all things, hopes all things, endures all things. Love never fails. But where there are prophecies, they will be done away with. Where there are various languages, they will cease. Where there is knowledge, it will be done away with. For we know in part, and we prophesy in part; but when that which is complete has come, then that which is partial will be done away with. When I was a child, I spoke as a child, I felt as a child, I thought as a child. Now that I have become a man, I have put away childish things. For now we see in a mirror, dimly, but then face to face. Now I know in part, but then I will know fully, even as I was also fully known. But now faith, hope, and love remain—these three. The greatest of these is love.

1 Corinthians 13:4-13 (WEB, my emphasis)

Now the serpent was more subtle *than any animal of the field which Yahweh God had made. He said to the woman, "Has God really said, 'You shall not eat of any tree of the garden?'"*
Genesis 3:1 (WEB, my emphasis)

A friend shared a recent snake adventure with me by email. I can't imagine that I have not vigorously shared with her how much I **HATE** snakes but her 'snake killing' story was an acceptable one to me because ... the snake **dies!** Now for all you 'circle of life' and reptile lovers out there who do not share my view of snakes, I want to say that I am aware of their function in the food chain but that does not diminish my negative view of them one wit!

The first time I read through the Bible I was very gratified to learn that God had chosen to give satan the physical body of a snake in my first introduction to him in Genesis. I thought it a rather appropriate type-casting myself! And God promises there that the serpent will be crushed. (Genesis 3:14-15) As I read on and found that a snake on a stick was an icon of healing in Numbers 21 after God used venomous snakes to bite and kill the disobedient Israelites, I turned the pages quickly and tried not to dwell on that story.

For a time in my spiritual life I gave too much time thinking about how much I hated **the subtle**, slimy serpent known as satan. I gave him far too much credit for what I saw in the world instead of acknowledging that we **allow** the consequences through our own poor choices. I truly allowed my hate to have more 'air' time than the **love** that was in me and in my life. Jesus said that all the power that He had been given was passed on to me to make disciples (Matthew 28). He also said that whatever I bound on earth would be bound in heaven. The snake is bound up and laid out so I can run over it with my spiritual tank! And run over it again, again, **again, again,** and **AGAIN!** How do I run over the snake?

I sing praise to my Lord! I raise my hands and dance for joy about what the Lord has done for me every day! I am **kind** to someone. I have **compassion** for someone. I **choose** to focus on Jesus and take time in my day to just sit at His feet and **listen**...quietly. I know you can think of some other ways that kick, toss, and generally give satan a nasty black eye!

1 Corinthians 10 says we do not wage war with weapons like guns and knives. We are in a spiritual war. There is no 'neutral' option. You can either follow Jesus and survive battles, win battles, and be on the **promised** victorious team – or you can be a part of the collateral damage. There is no staying out of the fray! Satan wants us under his feet! When we choose Jesus and follow Him – it is **satan** who is under our feet!!!

> *I heard a loud voice in heaven, saying, "Now the salvation, the power, and the Kingdom of our God, and the authority of his Christ has come; for the accuser of our brothers has been thrown down, who accuses them before our God day and night. They overcame him because of the Lamb's blood, and because of the word of their testimony. They didn't love their life, even to death. Therefore rejoice, heavens, and you who dwell in them. Woe to the earth and to the sea, because the devil has gone down to you, having great wrath, knowing that he has but a short time."*
> *Revelation 12:10-12 (WEB)*

First – I overcome anything satan thinks he can do because I am the child of the King and I testify about what Jesus has done in my life even to the point of dying with joy because that only brings me **eternal** life! Second, the devil is **really angry** and he doesn't have much time. OK. Then let's turn our backs on him and kick some dust in his face for as long as he has left!

My soul, wait in silence for God alone, for my expectation is from him.
He alone is my rock and my salvation, my fortress. I will not be shaken.
With God is my salvation and my honor. The rock of my strength, and my refuge, is in God.
Trust in him at all times, you people. Pour out your heart before him. God is a refuge for us.

Psalm 62:5-8 (WEB)

Yesterday was, on the surface, a really tough day for me. The voices of the world were definitely **LOUD, CLANGING CYMBALS!** I can take a fair amount of pressure but within an hour, I was in my office with the door closed, in tears. I went to my Lord and cried out to Him. I **needed** Him! Ten minutes later, I had the peace and the courage back to open the door and face the day.

Too often in the past, I have attempted to figure out the situation on my own. I have made lists. I have tossed and turned in my bed instead of sleeping. I have read books. Researched the internet. Now, all of these things are not bad ideas. I just didn't go to God **first!** When I turn to God first, my mind and my spirit calm and become more clear to receive the plan that **God** has. He may speak through a book or internet or my quiet mind that allows His voice to be heard!!!

The psalmist shows me, once again, the importance of my relationship with God. With a daily walk with Jesus, I **expect** Him to have the answers; have the plan. That **assurance** comes when I know very well the One to whom I am relying. I have a 'track record' with Him. I have the testimony of a 'cloud of witnesses'. (Many of you are in that crowd!) I trust Him.

Think of some of the many scenarios where you have seen people rise above their circumstance and walk with a quiet assurance. I have walk the halls of a cancer wing where children are connected to medications and parents are sitting beside their bed unable to take the pain or suffering from their child. Do they have questions like "Why?" Of course. I have seen so many extraordinary people after Hurricane Ivan came through my home town. The many that are **still** rebuilding after Hurricane Katrina in Louisiana and Hurricane Ike in Galveston, TX. What is the factor that can be identified in those who keep going and reach out to others even in their own 'poverty'? It is **faith** in God. Do they have questions like "Why?" Of course. Having questions does not mean a lack of faith. It does not indicate a lack of trust. If Jesus can question the Father's plan in Gethsemane and cry out His despair that the Father has left Him from the cross – I can too!

> When we walk with the Lord
>   in the light of His Word,
> What a glory He sheds on our way!
> While we do His good will, He abides with us still,
> And with all who will trust and obey.
>
> Not a shadow can rise, not a cloud in the skies,
> But His smile quickly drives it away;
> Not a doubt or a fear, not a sigh or a tear,
> Can abide while we trust and obey.
>
> Not a burden we bear, not a sorrow we share,
> But our toil He doth richly repay;
> Not a grief or a loss, not a frown or a cross,
> But is blessed if we trust and obey.
>
> But we never can prove the delights of His love—
> Until all on the altar we lay;

For the favor He shows, for the joy He bestows,
Are for them who will trust and obey.

Then in fellowship sweet we will sit at His feet,
Or we'll walk by His side in the way;
What He says we will do, where He sends we will go;
Never fear, only trust and obey.

"Trust and Obey"
by John Sammis, 1887 (public domain)

Prayer Choices   July 12

Paul, a prisoner of Christ Jesus, and Timothy our brother, to Philemon, our beloved fellow worker, to the beloved Apphia, to Archippus, our fellow soldier, and to the assembly in your house: Grace to you and peace from God our Father and the Lord Jesus Christ.
I thank my God always, making mention of you in my prayers, hearing of your love, and of the faith which you have toward the Lord Jesus, and toward all the saints; that the fellowship of your faith may become effective, in the knowledge of every good thing which is in us in Christ Jesus. For we have much joy and comfort in your love, because the hearts of the saints have been refreshed through you, brother.

Philemon 1-7 (WEB)

I want to take today and **really** encourage us all to **commit** to prayer. Paul is a great example of what prayer is all about and what it can be in your life. Paul is so open and continuous about his prayers. Every letter has a prayer or two or three in it. There are prayers of blessings. There are prayers of encouragement. There are prayers of **intense** supplication. There are prayers of great joy and thanksgiving. Paul's prayers often begin with an inner circle. He shares his own prayer for himself. Then people that he knows. The circle widens to the local church; then the whole Jewish community. The circle continues to widen.

Some may be able to do committed, focused prayer by just making up their mind to do so. I need visual aids. There are some wonderful options or ways to do personal prayer time. There are books written on the various ways that people do their prayer time. Recently I have been reading some of Philip Yancey's works and he shared some ideas that he has come upon. Three days a week he prays for family and friends. On alternate three days he prays for ministries and countries or more global concerns. And on the seventh day, he focusing only on himself, specifically asking God to examine him and teach him. He is quick to say that God has interrupted his plan, saying, "Oh, no, Philip, we are going to discuss **you** today!" Mr. Yancey also shared about using note cards with prayer needs written on cards that he has used especially when his life has gone through very busy times. The cards helped him get quiet and focus. I have used a 3-ring binder to write requests and left space for the answers to the prayers!

Some people use music as a vehicle to center and focus. Some use 'prayer chairs' or 'prayer rooms/closets'. Almost every person I have ever personally talked with about prayer has said that he/she came to that 'breakthrough' when they **committed to a time with God** and allowed very little to usurp that time.

Most 'good habits' do not come easily but instead come with a repetition of choice. Establishing a prayer habit builds prayer muscles. A quick scan on any given day to an online news service is enough to prove the need for prayer!

I am going to take time today to ask God to speak to my heart about His plan for my prayer life. I thank Him that He **wants** to meet with me. God **wants** to teach me and speak to me. He is waiting for me to make the time and make the choice.

"Because he has set his love on me, therefore I will deliver him.
I will set him on high, because he has known my name.
He will call on me, and I will answer him.
I will be with him in trouble. I will deliver him, and honor him.
I will satisfy him with long life, and show him my salvation."

Psalm 91:14-16 (WEB)

For many years this passage from Psalm 91 has been my prayer for my sons. I have claimed its promises for them. God is faithful to hear and answer.

God says that our love for Him brings on a response – He is watching and comes 'riding to the rescue' when we make choices that get us in trouble! When we take the stand that we only recognize Him as Lord in our lives, **He** stands over us like a shield of protection! When we call and cry out to Him, He answers. **He answers!** When troubles come (And they will. We can guarantee that!), God will already be there. He will be a tangible presence in the trouble that will lead us out of the trouble. He will respect and admire us because in that trouble, we turned to Him and expected Him to be there. We turned in the best direction! God will give me a life-span that has no end! **He** will show me eternity!

My son, James, died in 2004 at age 17. James' life continues on through people who, because of his life-testimony, made a choice to live **their** lives with Jesus. They saw God's courage and strength in James' life and said, "I want some of that!" "I **need** some of that!" James is having a long life!

My son, John, continues to write his legacy. He is walking his life in front of his own sons, showing them an example of what it is to be God's man in this world. It is about showing your children that you are weak but God will keep His promises and make you strong! It is turning to God for wisdom and direction in your life and doing what He says even when you can't see the 'why' of it.

> *...whatever things are true, whatever things are honorable, whatever things are just, whatever things are pure, whatever things are lovely, whatever things are of good report; if there is any virtue, and if there is any praise, think about these things. The things which you learned, received, heard, and saw in me: do these things, and the God of peace will be with you.*
>
> *Philippians 4:8-9 (WEB)*

This has been my Scripture for my daughter, Janet. She has been given a **gift** of faith. I sometimes think that is a difficult gift to carry because it may mean that she **believes** when everyone around thinks it can't possibly happen! I believe God put this passage in my heart to use as a prayer that she would keep her focus on Him and not be distracted.

What words of God do you pray over your children? Your spouse? No matter how young or old they may be...God is **faithful** and a **keeper of His promises.** Ask God to direct your heart to His words for His children.

Blessings   July 14

> *"I pray that the LORD will bless and protect you, and that he will show you mercy and kindness. May the LORD be good to you and give you peace."*
>
> *Numbers 6:24-26 (CEV)*

Did you grow up in a home where **'The Blessing'** was said before every meal? I did. It was a specific prayer that we said every meal, every day. And that is OK except by the time I was old enough to understand the prayer it had become such a 'habit' that I didn't **listen** and ask the blessing from my heart.

My mother had set the example but I didn't follow. It's wonderful to see my children encourage my grandchildren to pray their own blessings. I got a 'eaves-dropping' recording from my daughter the other night. My granddaughter was praying before she went to sleep...doing her "...and God bless...". She was praying specifically for her "Uncle John" that he would do well in a baseball game he was going to pitch in her home town the next night. He was on her heart because she was going to see him soon. At one point, I think her daddy was helping her with some words and she said, "Stop, Daddy! You're messing up my prayer!" We have all laughed at that but it certainly preaches to all of us. Remember how Jesus told us to have the faith of a child? May we remember that God hears the prayer of our hearts (even if words fail us!) and answers well!

A blessing is a prayer that leaves out manipulation and personal agenda and instead asks God to pour out His gifts upon His child (or children). The example of this prayer given by God to Moses and addressed to the Levites asks for such good stuff! When praying for someone no matter what the specific need, including these elements is asking for a double blessing, isn't it? When someone has, say, a health need, lifting that need to God and being specific as the Holy Sprit leads and then asking God to protect and show mercy and kindness and goodness and cover that person with His peace – that is truly asking God to give more than they could ask or imagine!

> *[Jesus said,] "But I tell you who hear: love your enemies, do good to those who hate you, bless those who curse you, and pray for those who mistreat you."*
>
> *Luke 6:27-28 (WEB)*

Jesus' words are never – careless. He always says what He means. I may not always understand it the way Jesus means but maybe His first phrase here gives me a clue about that! "you who hear me". Do I want to hear what Jesus says? In this case, the words that I have heard and received about 'blessings' even goes for those people in my life who hate me, dislike me, irritate me, bug me, and even mistreat those I love. Yes, do I **really** want to hear that?

> [Jesus said,] *If you love those who love you, what credit is that to you? For even sinners love those who love them. If you do good to those who do good to you, what credit is that to you? For even sinners do the same. If you lend to those from whom you hope to receive, what credit is that to you? Even sinners lend to sinners, to receive back as much. But love your enemies, and do good, and lend, expecting nothing back; and your reward will be great, and you will be children of the Most High; for he is kind toward the unthankful and evil. Therefore be merciful, even as your Father is also merciful.*
>
> Luke 6:32-36 (WEB)

Jesus **asks** more of me. Jesus **gives** more **to** me. He gives me **all that I need** to be obedient and glorify the Father. It comes down to a choice on my part. It comes down to my flesh. There aren't many in the 'enemy' category, thank my Lord, but they do exist. What healing, what joy, what heavenly peace comes to me when I make the choice and ask the Holy Spirit to give me what I need so I can pray blessings over **all!**

Jesus Came   July 15

> [Jesus said,] *"For the Son of Man came to seek and to save that which was lost."*
>
> Luke 19:10 (WEB)

Look at that profound and yet beautiful statement: Jesus came to **see**k and **save** what **was** lost. Jesus came as a man. I can not even understand the many reasons why Jesus came **fully** man and **fully** God. I can't really wrap my mind around what that means much less the 'why' of it. I do know that God Himself came here on earth as a man. He **ha**d to sleep. He **had** to eat. He **had** to earn a wage. He **had** to love – some people easier than others maybe in His humanness! He **had** to grieve when His earthly father, Joseph, died. He **had** to suffer physically the whipping and crucifixion. He **had** to suffer the scorn of His family and His church. Jesus did all of this (and more!) because of love. Love that I did not deserve or ask Him to give. Love that had He asked I probably would have refused it. Up until the age of 40, I was convinced that I could handle (and should handle) my life and if I just worked hard and had some 'breaks' from fate – my life and that of my family would be **OK**. I signed up for church. That was an important box to be checked. I like to **do** stuff and I could use my expertise and talents there. I did not accept free gifts. Church was a place to pay my dues so I stayed on God's good side so He would like me.

Jesus came to find me even when I did not know I was lost and **needed** saving. And there is also the **fact** that there were times I did know I was so very unhappy (lost) but still thought I could make it better. I should be able to do this!

"He was there all the time. Waiting patiently in line..." – Gary S. Paxton, 1975

Jesus came and when I stopped digging that hole and reached out my hand; sweaty and dirty like I was, helpless to do anything more on my own, Jesus' hand was there waiting to grasp mine and lift me up. I still get sweaty and dirty when I step off the path but that is for another day.

Thank You, Jesus. Thank You. You love me even when I am most unlovable. You see me as I can be and show me the way – walking before me. Thank You. Those are my words for today: Thank You.

Being asked by the Pharisees when the Kingdom of God would come, he [Jesus] answered them, 'The Kingdom of God doesn't come with observation; 17:21 neither will they say, 'Look, here!' or, 'Look, there!' for behold, the Kingdom of God is within you."
Luke 17:20-21 (WEB, my emphasis)

Yesterday Jesus was speaking about how much He loved me – even when I didn't ask and couldn't earn His love. Today, Jesus took His love a step further and says He has picked me (and you) to **be** His Kingdom.

Jesus says the Kingdom, in its glory and as He promised, will not come with my keen religious knowledge and/or prophecy of what is to come or should happen. In fact, Jesus says that no one will be able to say "Here it is!" or "There it is!" because –

Therefore if anyone is in Christ, he is a new *creation. The old things have passed away. Behold, all things have become* new. *But all things are of God, who reconciled us to himself through Jesus Christ, and* gave *to us the ministry of reconciliation; namely, that God was in Christ reconciling the world to himself, not reckoning to them their trespasses,* [not giving us what we deserved!] *and having* committed to us *the word of reconciliation. We are therefore ambassadors on behalf of Christ, as though God were entreating by us:* we beg you *on behalf of Christ,* be reconciled to God. *For him* [Jesus] *who knew no sin he* [the Father] *made to be sin on our behalf; so that* in him *we might become the righteousness of God* [in right relationship with God].
2 Corinthians 5:17-21 (WEB, my emphasis and paraphrase)

Paul said, it well. God had no Plan B. It was God's plan all along to come in the flesh – as man – and be the only sacrifice that could cover my sins so that I could be Jesus' ambassador; His representative 2000 years later to others. **I am** the representative of **God's Kingdom! ME!** Less than perfect – still in need of forgiveness when – after choosing to follow Jesus in 1995 (and I haven't changed my mind!) – I still need Jesus to bring me back to His chosen path for me when I wander off. How far have I wandered since 1995? (If you could see me right now you would see me blush, roll my eyes, and drop my head in shame.)

If I reference the Bible, the writers, taking down God's words for me, do not list sins as "little" or "big", do they?

Jesus said, He did not get rid of the Law but He tried to get me to understand that sin is not just my actions but more about my heart. (Matthew 5) Paul comes along in Galations 5 and while he gives a list of what is my sinful nature and how that reflects my life, Paul is trying to say what Jesus said, "Jody, it's about what is in your heart that builds my Kingdom. If your heart is sold out to me first, your life on earth despite all its imperfections will build My Kingdom."

How the Kingdom grows in me is for tomorrow.

"The Kingdom of Heaven is like..." July 17

"The Kingdom of Heaven is like..."

Matthew 13:24 (WEB)

Yesterday I learned that the Kingdom of Heaven is **in** me even though I am 'way imperfect! Today, God led me to the parables in Matthew 13 to read how Jesus **tries** to tell what the Kingdom of Heaven is **like**. Take out your Bible and join me in Matthew 13:

vv. 24-30 God sows His good Word in my heart. He teaches me so that good fruit (check Galatians 5) will grow in me. The enemy also sows seeds; destructive seeds. God does not prevent the seeds from being sown. He could but He doesn't.

Remember in Matthew 5 that Jesus even said that the sun and rain comes to evil **and** good. Not until Judgment Day does sifting harvest occur.

vv. 31-32 God may call me to the smallest of jobs by the world's standard but God can take that small, insignificant seed and make it **BIG** in His Kingdom.

vv. 33 The yeast of God's goodness can work all through me and affect everything that I do. Remember Jesus also **warned** that yeast **not** of Him can also affect me. (yeast of the Pharisees, Luke 12:1)

vv. 44-45 When you find the treasure in your walk with God – it is worth whatever the price. You may think you have lost the big home, many clothes, big vacations, but you will find what will never rust or decay in Jesus.

vv. 47-50 The Kingdom of Heaven has **all kinds** of fish. Jesus casts His net wide and long. It is at Judgment Day that the fish will be divided, until then, we are all together!

vv. 52 Jesus ends this series of parables telling us that **in the storeroom** we bring out new and old treasures. In my heart, Jesus will bring treasures that have remained fresh for 2000 years. He will also bring new treasures that do not **replace** the old but, in fact, bring a bountiful harvest in my heart.

The Kingdom of Heaven is here and now in me and that means it is not the perfection that it will become when Jesus comes as King of Kings. How the Kingdom will live and grow in me depends on my choices. All that I need to glorify God's Kingdom is available to me – but will I choose to follow Jesus and build the Kingdom by His example and choose my own plan? Seems like a no brain-er but in the choices there will be a 'letting go' of what may be easy and what may be expected by the world.

The Kingdom of Heaven – it's where there is God's grace and mercy. **Is** it in me?

Jesus answered, "My Kingdom is not of this world. If my Kingdom were of this world, then my servants would fight, that I wouldn't be delivered to the Jews. But now my Kingdom is not from here."
Pilate therefore said to him, "Are you a king then?"
Jesus answered, "You say that I am a king. For this reason I have been born, and for this reason I have come into the world, that I should testify to the truth. *Everyone who is of the truth listens to my voice."*
Pilate said to him, "What is truth?"

John 18: 36-38 (WEB, my emphasis)

This week Jesus has been speaking to me about the Kingdom of Heaven. Frankly, He is trying to get me to lift my eyes off myself and consider how I can live by Kingdom principles.

One of those principles is about truth. Pilate asked, as many philosophers before him and to the present ask, "What is truth?" Some might say that truth is reality. It is what I can see and/or touch. Truth is much more than that. It is more than a transient moment. Truth should be something that guides how I live.

"You will know the truth, and the truth will make you free."

John 8:32 (WEB)

When I know something to be true, it can be part of a revelation that   I begin to know for what reason I am here.

Jesus is a truth to me. Someone reading this may dismiss that statement because they feel I am unable to **prove** Jesus and His reason that He came to seek and save the lost and to testify to that truth. Jesus is as real to me as my husband. His impact on me has been life-changing and forever-changing. I **was** lost. I am no longer. I don't have to prove anything more. You would have to **dis**-prove it to me! The truth of Jesus and that which He has shared with me has set me free.

A disciple of Jesus is more than a Believer. It is making a **daily choice** to live a Kingdom of Heaven life in this world. It is walking that choice out as a living testimony to what Jesus is doing today.

One of my favorite books is *The Nun's Story* by Kathryn Hulme. (Audrey Hepburn starred in the movie.) It is the story of the life of a young girl during WWII, who made the decision to become a nun and the subsequent spiritual battle she wages to become the Bride of Christ that is demanded of her. She is told that it is her quest to become so perfect in the Living Rule (the life of service, humility, and chastity to which she has chosen) that a novice coming into the life could follow her and be following what is asked.

Jesus shows me His perfection and His standard is the only one I should follow as perfect. My walk is far from perfection. It is an imperfect testimony that (I pray) says to anyone looking at me: I walk beside my Savior, humble that He would invite me to do so and joyous that He has given me a Kingdom of Heaven life that can **never** be destroyed.

3,000 New Believers   July 19

> *But Peter, standing up with the eleven, lifted up his voice, and spoke out to them,...*
>
> *Acts 2:14 (WEB)*

A fisherman, considered to be 'illiterate' by the society of his time since he probably wasn't able to read the Torah and spoke Aramaic, stood up in front of "Jews from every nation under heaven" (Acts 2:5) and spoke! No, **preached!** Peter **filled with the Holy Spirit** did not hesitate, did not stutter or stammer. He opened his mouth – and people listened! And what did Peter say in this inspired sermon?

- Peter tried to explain what had happened. He told the crowd that neither he nor the other eleven were drunk. Why do you think the crowd thought they were drunk? Were they smiling and laughing? Were they dancing in the streets and leaping for joy? Hmmm.

- Peter quoted the prophet, Joel, reminding the Jews of God's promises. He said that church as usual was no longer going to be the usual! There would be God's Spirit **present** among the Believers and they would be **seeing** 'stuff' that may be a little…unsettling? Would 'freaky' be too harsh a word? And people who call on Jehovah God as Lord will be saved from eternal destruction!

- **God is alive!** He is active and present in their lives. He came to earth and cannot be killed. **He is alive!**

The people "were cut to the heart" (Acts 2:37). They realized their sinfulness and **repented**. 'Repent' means to turn away and not do that any more! The moment that you put down your pride and allow the truth of God to enter in…it's overwhelming! It's honestly seeing what you are – a sinner – and it's also receiving that undeserved love and forgiveness…**grace and mercy** …and just **leaping for joy** – inside and out!

Peter warned and pleaded with the people to come and make a decision to **believe** and **live** their lives for God! "Save yourselves from this corrupt generation." (Acts 2:40 NIV) In other words, stop going the way of the world and choose a different path – God's path! Peter pointed to the way to **life!**

I don't know how many were there but **3,000** of them accepted what Peter was saying and got baptized and were added to the number of Believers. There isn't a pastor or evangelist that wouldn't be excited about bringing 3,000 people to know God in one day! WOW!

What happened next? What would your church do next if 3,000 people came through your doors and said, "We believe in Jesus Christ?" Would you know what to do next? We'll look at that tomorrow. Meanwhile, take a few minutes and read Joel 2 for your reading today.

Devoted to God   July 20

They continued steadfastly in the apostles' teaching and fellowship, in the breaking of bread, and prayer.

Acts 2:42 (WEB)

I have frequently heard in conversations with fellow Believers that we would "love to see our church look like the first church after Pentecost". We would love to attend such a church…but are we willing to do what they did?

This group of Believers came together daily. **Daily! DAILY!** Most of us are not **really** willing to do that. When our church has revival services we can't make the priority to come every night for **four** nights! (Sunday-Wednesday) We complain if our Sunday service lasts more than an hour. We whine (or ignore) when small group study involves 'homework'! The words in this passage say that the Believers were **devoted** to the teaching. What does that mean? "Well, if we had a 'Peter' teaching us we would be committed and loyal to that teaching too!" There is **always** an excuse that can be found for not being faithful to the teaching that **God** has provided us! Too often it is not a lack of good teaching but a lack of investment from the student! If I am stepping on toes today – remember that God stepped on **mine** first!

34

This group of Believers also broke bread together. They had fellowship. They remembered that Jesus told them that when they came together in unity, breaking the basic – like bread – that He would be there with them. On any given week, with whom do we break bread? Do we remember to acknowledge that Jesus is there? Is our conversation something that He would want to be a part? Do we spend time **building up the Body** or tearing it down in our conversations?

This group of Believers came together daily to **pray!** Personal prayer **and** corporate prayer was a priority! Recently my daughter told me that their pastor decided not to have their usual Saturday evening service and their Sunday service. There was a need to pray for two families who were battling very serious illness. There was a need and so the group of Believers made meeting that need a priority. Are we willing to suspend the 'usual' order of worship to meet the needs of the Body or are we too concerned about what others – even a visitor – might think? If I was a visitor, I might not know the ones who had the need but I would be pretty impressed with a church who was willing to meet that need!

> *The Lord added to the assembly day by day those who were being saved.*
>
> *Acts 2:47 (WEB, emphasis mine)*

Well, duh! Do you think? When we 'allow' **God** to be the leader of the church then good things happen. When we stop trying to figure out and over-think and make a program fit and just let **God** do the figuring and the planning and the fitting – then good things happen. **God** gets the credit nor the program or the person. **God.** We turn our hearts to God. We give Him our time and priorities. We praise Him in all things. The world is looking for us to be **really** and **truly** sold out to God! No more straddling the fence but firmly on God's side. Let us be **devoted to God.**

The heavens declare the glory of God. The expanse shows his handiwork.

Day after day they pour forth speech, and night after night they display knowledge.

There is no speech nor language, where their voice is not heard.

Their voice has gone out through all the earth, their words to the end of the world.

In them he has set a tent for the sun, which is as a bridegroom coming out of his room,

like a strong man rejoicing to run his course.

His going forth is from the end of the heavens, his circuit to its ends;

There is nothing hidden from its heat.

Yahweh's law is perfect, restoring the soul. Yahweh's testimony is sure, making wise the simple.

Yahweh's precepts are right, rejoicing the heart. Yahweh's commandment is pure, enlightening the eyes.

The fear of Yahweh is clean, enduring forever. Yahweh's ordinances are true, and righteous altogether.

More to be desired are they than gold, yes, than much fine gold;

sweeter also than honey and the extract of the honeycomb.

Moreover by them is your servant warned. In keeping them there is great reward.

Psalm 19:1-11 (WEB)

When I work on the weekend and have a slow time I go to the online Bible (www.ebible.org) and read usually the psalms. I am not gifted to write poetry but, praise God, I can appreciate it!

If you haven't taken time to sit outside and look at the sky, I hope you will take some time this week and do so. Wherever you live, the beauty of the night sky with the stars winking against the dark expanse is time in a beautiful sanctuary uniquely created each evening by our Lord. And then there is the daylight when clouds move softly through or quickly darken as a storm moves in. Even the flash and crack of thunder and lightening are magnificent in their power. I enjoy a storm as I watch through the window in the safety of my home.

Taking the time to look and marvel at the creation of God is a time of worship and encouragement. It affirms to me the reality and supremacy of my Creator and God. I connect to the presence of God and arrive at a new level of awareness that He is Elohim, mighty God, and yet knows me as His child.

The writer of this psalm is not **just** looking at the beauty. The writer is also celebrating the law, statues, precepts, commands, and ordinances of our God. Now what **do** all of those words mean? There are **books** written about that! And for me, when all is written and said, it matters what **God** says to **me** about those words and how that will affect the life He has for me to live. So here is what I have learned:

- God's Law – to the Jews, the Torah, teaches, reviving my life in Him. It is the parental side of God **trying** to teach me right from wrong.

- God's statues – They are **His** testimony to who and what He is. They are to be trusted and give wisdom to anyone who has ears to hear.

- God's precepts – The principles that I can learn as God teaches me. His principles are written on my heart.

- God's commands – These are the "mitzvahs", the good deeds of my Lord. They are the light in a dark world; even a revelation.

- God's ordinances – God's judgment is always **just**. God has no prejudice or bias. God is the only judge.

Depending on the translation you read, different words are used in the verses we have meditated on today. But all translations use five different words to describe these God-words. As I read and spoke with Henry about the Hebrew words that the words tried to describe in their translation, I understood that finite (limiting) words will never be able to completely describe our infinite God! However limiting, I came away from this psalm with new views and felt closer to my God. And that is what I believe God wants for me – to be closer to Him.

More of God's Gifts   July 22

More to be desired are they than gold, yes, than much fine gold;
sweeter also than honey and the extract of the honeycomb.
Moreover by them is your servant warned. In keeping them
there is great reward.
Who can discern his errors? Forgive me from hidden errors.
Keep back your servant also from presumptuous sins. Let
them not have dominion over me.
Then I will be upright. I will be blameless and innocent of great
transgression.
Let the words of my mouth and the meditation of my heart
be acceptable in your sight,
Yahweh, my rock, and my redeemer.

Psalm 19:10-14 (WEB)

Yesterday I studied the first 9 verses of this psalm and learned more about how much God loves **and** cares about me. He desires so much for me to be in a close relationship with Him that He teaches me through His many faceted ways. I spent some time yesterday looking at clouds and then the stars last night and thought some more about God's magnificence.

The psalmist tells me that God's commands, ordinances,

precepts, laws, and statues are better than **gold!** That in their wisdom I am warned; I am guided in Jesus' path that leads to more than I could ask or imagine! I do not start out to drive somewhere I have never been without first reading the directions, do I? Then spending time studying and learning God's way seems like wisdom to me!

Then the psalmist asks a pointed, right-on-the-point question: Who knows his/her own errors? I thought it was interesting that the question did not use the word 'sins' but said 'errors'. It occurs to me that to be able to know my errors is to have an opportunity for **correction** that will come **before** sin! God's ways will help me to **avoid** the sin that can so easily tangle me up! (Hebrews 12) And when my 'error' comes because I ignored the warnings or just plain take a wrong turn – I am reminded that God's mercy, His forgiveness, is there. It has no limitation. Because of Jesus' sacrifice, there is no 'error'; there is no 'sin' that God will not forgive. Am I unworthy of such love? Well, duh. Again, it is the gift of Jesus, my Savior, that tilts the scales.

The last verse is familiar. It is one that I have repeated on many occasions. I will be saying it more often. I have a new perspective on what the words means to me.

Lord, may Your words that I think about and speak be pleasing to You because I speak and think of them often. In the midst of whatever storm or rocky path that I navigate, You and You alone, are my Rock and my Redeemer. Thank You, Lord, for these gifts. It is in Jesus' name I pray, Amen.

Consequences   July 23

> *The children of Israel* again *did that which was evil in the sight of Yahweh, when Ehud was dead. 4:2 Yahweh sold them into the hand of Jabin king of Canaan,...*
>
> Judges 4:1-2 (WEB, my emphasis)

For the most part of my 'early' Christian years, I read the New Testament. I've never been a history buff and, generally, I am not a person who looks back. I look forward and anticipate what is to come…not what has been. So the Old Testament has never held much an appeal. But there is something to be learned from history…so that I don't repeat it.

It is not always 'fun' to talk about consequences of our actions. No child wants to be disciplined. If a child doesn't do their homework and as a consequence is not allowed to go to a football game on Friday night **that** is not fun! However, as much as we may not want to study this passage, learning about consequences when we want to grow spiritually means that we recognize that there is a need to mature; to **grow up!** God, our very loving Father, wants us to grow up. He does it with His never-ending love **and** with consequences when we choose not to be obedient. The Israelites had been given many chances to make choices and they continued to want it **their way!**

I admit that I have also tried to convince myself that I do not always know what God **really** wants me to do. Yes I do. It's not as complicated as I try to make it. Jesus said to love God, love my neighbor, and love myself. Everything else is connected to those two simple commands. Paul said to think about those things that are noble, right, pure, lovely, excellent, admirable, and praiseworthy. (Philippians 4:8) He also said that if what I am doing produces "fruit" like love, joy, peace, patience, kindness, goodness, faithfulness, gentleness, and self-control – then I am living my life with God's Spirit. (Galatians 5:22-23) These are good "tests" to know the "good" and "avoid every…evil". (1 Thessalonians 5:21-22) Paul also said that he, too, **knew** what he was supposed to do but that he struggled **not** to do what he **knew** he shouldn't (Romans 7:15). Paul knew that if he just stopped trying to be so right by his own strength and in his own pride and got weak and humble – God would show forth His strength and Paul would follow God's way.

I've shared the story often about my oldest son, John, when he was just a toddler. He was playing on the kitchen floor while I was cooking one day. I had something baking in the oven and John continued to want to touch the oven door. I told him **"NO!"** in a stern voice but he tried again. I slapped his little hand and said **"NO!"** once more. I turned to the sink and saw him move toward the stove once more. I knew if he touched the oven he would hurt his fingers but it wouldn't cause a third-degree burn...so I didn't stop him the third time. Of course he cried and looked at me with such reproach like "Mama, how **could** you **let** me do that?!!" I gathered him up and stuck his fingers in a cold ice bath and rocked him, probably gave him a sippee cup of juice until all his tears were dry. And my tears, too. I **hated** he had to hurt but he learned a consequence then would help him to grow and learn that there **are** consequences to disobedience.

Our Lord is **so loving** and **so perfect** as my Father. He wants me to grow up and grow closer to Him. He would rather that I grow through love but He is willing to use consequences so that I can become all that He has created me to be!

Blessed is the man who trusts in Yahweh, and whose trust Yahweh is. For he shall be as a tree planted by the waters, who spreads out its roots by the river, and shall not fear when heat comes, but its leaf shall be green; and shall not be careful in the year of drought, neither shall cease from yielding fruit.

Jeremiah 17:7-8 (WEB)

God's Love – Stand in it! July 24

Through Silvanus, our faithful brother, as I consider him, I have written to you briefly, exhorting, and testifying that this is the true grace of God in which you stand. *1 Peter 5:12 (WEB)*

In my reading of Peter, he certainly seems very driven; someone who did not speak gently or even politely. And yet here Peter says that he needed Silas' help to to write. Peter was a fisherman and in those days may not have had much of an opportunity to receive education. He may have needed Silas to write so that what he was hearing in his spirit or feeling in his heart could be put into language that is readily available and understandable.

Unlike Paul, Peter's letters **were** more to the point and matter of fact. In this one verse, Peter sums it up: "I wrote you a few words to encourage you and as a testimony to the truth of God's love. STAND FIRM in that LOVE!"

My heart is "strangely warmed" as John Wesley said, by Peter's words. God's love is a **fact**. It is a fact that I can stand in when the winds of adversity blow! It is a fact that I can stand in when no one else brings their love my way without conditions! It is a fact that I can stand on when I have nothing else on which to stand. If I fell I have lost everything – I am still loved by God.

God's love is a burst of encouragement in a draining world. I have spoken about how I have noticed the stars and the clouds and their beauty. God's love is in those clouds and stars. I have stood and watched in awe as thousands of gallons of water rush over Niagara Falls and thought what it must have been like for those first Indians. They were walking through the trees wondering what was the sound that seem to grow into a louder roar. Then they followed a large river until – they beheld those magnificent falls. They must have fallen down on their faces in fear and awe! Thousands of years later, I too stood there and wept, not in fear, but in wonder of my Creator who made those Falls just for the good pleasure of His children! God who made the falls so great can still hold them in His hand! And He can also hold my heart ever so gently in His hand. Neither His power nor His gentleness has no end!

How GREAT is our Lord and WORTHY to be praise! Thank You, Lord, for Your extravagant, unsurpassed love!

Thank You that You care for me in every minute, even when I am asleep or any other time that I am unaware. Thank You, Lord. Thank You! I will STAND today in Your Love! May the words that I speak and the thoughts that keep today – be pleasing to You, in Jesus' name I pray. Amen.

Consider Carefully   July 25

He [Jesus] *said to them, "Take heed what you hear. With whatever measure you measure, it will be measured to you, and more will be given to you who hear. For whoever has, to him will more be given, and he who doesn't have, even that which he has will be taken away from him."*

Mark 4:24-25 (WEB)

I have been told that Mark uses phrases like this starting one to signify that Jesus was saying, "Heads up! Listen up! I am about to say something really important!" I think what Jesus said next is very important. It is a principal about how I live my life **but** I do **not** think it is about

$$$!!! How many people are going to stop reading this or at a minimum are disappointed that I don't think it's about money?

Jesus wasn't about money. He wasn't about laying up treasures here on earth, was He? (Matthew 6:19) Jesus said that I was to think about my **eternal** bank account. Jesus wanted me to live my life with the focus being on following His example and building God's kingdom. When I extend grace to others as God has extended to me, God says, **"YEAH!"** and offers a High 5! When I remember how forgiving God has been to me and I extend that forgiveness to others, God lifts me up on His shoulders! And so God will give **more.** God gives and gives! He gives gifts in abundance! He gives whatever I will need to accomplish His plan in abundance. Let me give a personal example:

When Henry and I got married, many were more than a little surprised because we are so very different. But God...well, He's a good matchmaker! He was thinking about Kingdom partnerships! Henry is a visionary. He sees a big picture. He thinks in terms of the Church. I am an administrator. I am a detail person that sees the steps to make a conference happen. However, in the last nine years, I think Henry and I have both learned that our 'gifts' do not have hard, sharp lines of separation. God saw us as two who would become one. We have learned to work together to make something happen. We continue to learn from God on how we can grow together better! When we choose to use the gifts that God has given us – He gives more! IF we neglect or do not use our gifts – God gives them to someone else. He is not going to waste His gifts.

Every day we have an opportunity to do Kingdom work. It may be encouraging a co-worker or just listening. If you tell someone you are going to be praying for them...do it! A one sentence prayer right then can lift a person from despair and break the lie that they are alone or the only one who is having this particular problem. It may be doing that 'something extra' for our own family. It's bringing home a $5 bouquet of daisies...just because...for a spouse or a child. It's getting up from the table first and taking dishes to the washer or becoming the washer, without being told. Sending a card to someone—even an e-card! There was a woman in my church that, at her funeral, literally 100 people or more, raised their hand that they had received a card from her at a **moment** when no one else knew but God that they were going through difficulties. The woman sent a card and totally changed lives. Is that a gift? Absolutely! I believe that for every prophet in the Church, we need 4-6 encouragers.

"Consider carefully what you hear," Jesus says. I want to hear what Jesus says every day. I want to hear Him and then consider carefully what His words are and how they are to move me. Consider carefully what God is saying to you today.

Learning Obedience   July 26

..."*Go to your house, to your friends, and tell them what great things the Lord has done for you, and how he had mercy on you.*" *Mark 5:19 (WEB)*

He strictly ordered them that no one should know this,... Mark 5:43 (WEB)

These Scriptures are from two stories of miraculous healings. The first is the demon-possessed man that ran through the tombs in the region of Gerasenes. Jesus commands the demons calling themselves Legion to come out of the man and sends the demons into a herd of pigs. The man is so overjoyed and thankful for what God has done that he wants to follow and serve Jesus. Jesus says "No" and "Go tell". The second is the story of Jairus the centurion's daughter who dies before Jesus can arrive. Jesus takes only Peter, James, and John with Him on this 'mission'. He sends the wailers out of the room, leaving only the parents and the three disciples. After the child comes back to life Mark and Luke both state that Jesus ordered the five not to talk about what happened. (Luke 8:56)   Matthew, however, does not say that but says that the news spread throughout the region. (Matthew 9:26)   I would think that all three gospels tell the story: Jesus said not to tell but a parent would have difficulty not telling the story of how their child was restored to them! And this is where Jesus led me today.

Obedience. Using this specific order from God: to tell or nor to tell, Jesus shows that because God sees the **Big Picture** there are times He may tell me to speak and there are times He may say, "Be quiet!"   God can see the 'ripple-effect' of my actions. He can see when I share what He has done in my life how Janey Smith or Louis Leech will react. God understands the **timing** of things. His eyes look much farther into the future than my eyes can. It is just as disobedient **to testify** as it is **not to testify** if God has not given the command. Especially in testifying I believe that when God sends His Spirit before me to touch, to 'tenderize' people's hearts that will allow His word in my testimony to fall on fertile ground and grow into something bigger than I can imagine.

Remember Pentecost? Remember how the fisherman, Peter, stood up in front of Jews from all over the world, unafraid, and told them about the Living Christ? By the **power of God's Spirit**, 3,000 people had open hearts to receive the Good News of the Messiah. It was not Peter's great words but God's great power running **through** Peter that brought those 3,000 to eternal salvation. If Peter had spoke outside God's plan, he would have died.

And then there was Stephen. He also spoke with God's Spirit in God's timing and he **was** stoned to death. God's plan is perfect and the result will always be good. Stephen did not 'lose' that day. He 'won' his reward. When we walk in God's will, we never lose. We only win eternity for ourselves and others.

How do we know when to speak or not? We build our relationship with God so that we **know** His voice and are **open** to His answer…not confined by our own pre-conceived idea of how God should use us and work. We build, day by day, prayer by prayer, word by studied word, until like any child, we can hear our Father's voice amidst all the other voices in our life. Listen. Learn. Respond in obedience, "Speak, Lord. Your servant is listening."

There were shepherds in the same country staying in the field, and keeping watch by night over their flock. Behold, an angel of the Lord stood by them, and the glory of the Lord shone around them, and they were terrified.

Luke 2:8-9 (WEB)

I know it is July but I recently noticed several stores having "Christmas in July" sales so I thought I would read the Christmas Story again today. And I found a 'gold nugget' from God!

Here are the shepherds out in the field, in the middle of the night, and they are watching sheep. I don't know a lot about sheep but I would think that the night shift in the life of a shepherd would be **dull.** Shepherds want the night to be dull! Any disturbance is going to involve carnivorous animals and/or poachers! The disturbance that night was like **nothing** they could have imagined!

"Change always brings fear before it brings faith." (Max Lucado, God Came Near, ISBN: 0849944546)

True! When God is leading me into a deeper level of faith, it is going to be characterized by change. Faith does not grow in my comfort zone! Faith grows in the garden of adversity that is found on the craggy slope of my fear. It is the moment when I wonder, **"Where are You, God??!"** There is a a few minutes or a few hours or a few days when I keep looking at myself and do not turn to God and the testimony of His Word or His actions in the lives of others – in my own life! Even in the **glory of the Lord,** the shepherds are **terrified.** Or maybe it is because of the glory that they are afraid.

The angel said to them, 'Don't be afraid, for behold, I bring you good news of great joy which will be to all the people. For there is born to you, this day, in the city of David, a Savior, who is Christ the Lord. vv. 10-11 (WEB)

As I turn to the Lord and **see** His glory, it is important that I listen to God's messengers and not – the other guy who will try to whisper hateful, destructive garbage into my ear. **"Do not be afraid!"** God wants to give me Good News! God wants me to draw closer to Jesus and be the disciple that He has envisioned me to be! Jesus said that He wants me to have a **full** (or abundant) **life**. (John 10:10) What does that mean to God? What does it mean to me? The answer to that comes as I spend time with God listening! Listening to God but also listening to what He has planted in my heart.

In faith I find the assurance about what I am hoping for; even those things I have not yet seen.   Hebrews 11:1 (my paraphrase)

Is the wind of change – **faith** – blowing through your life today??!

Clean House   July 28

[Jesus said,] "The unclean spirit, when he has gone out of the man, passes through dry places, seeking rest, and finding none, he says, 'I will turn back to my house from which I came out.' 11:25 When he returns, he finds it swept and put in order. 11:26 Then he goes, and takes seven other spirits more evil than himself, and they enter in and dwell there. The last state of that man becomes worse than the first."

Luke 11:24-26 (WEB)

A young man stood up one night in the church I was attending and told his story about how he had been miraculously set free from alcoholism some years before. He began to attend church regularly, going to Bible study, and even played on the church softball team. He thought he had 'arrived' in a spiritual

48

safe haven. He missed a Sunday here and there. Didn't go to Bible study during the summer months…thought he would take a vacation and relax. "I didn't know what a slippery slope I stepped on!" He began to drink again, almost dying in an alcoholic overdose.

Too often in the last years, since I made my commitment to Jesus, I, too, have stepped on to the slope that the young man described. My story may not seem as dramatic but my footsteps were no less scary! I thought I could **relax** and not take my spiritual health **too seriously**. I was a **mature Christian**. I knew my Bible. I knew what my Lord's voice sounded like. **I knew.**

Jesus' metaphor is very descriptive and clear. When I **choose** to clean my life and sweep out the **junk** in my life, I have to **fill it** with the Holy Spirit. I need to **grow** fruit: love, joy, peace, patience, kindness, goodness, faithfulness, gentleness and self-control. (Galatians 5:22-23) **But** if I am living a life like Christ then I am giving **out** that fruit and I have to restock my shelves! I have to stay actively connected to the Living Vine! I have to drink in the Spirit's Living Water and consume the Fresh Bread of God's Word.

Let us take our spiritual life even more seriously than we do our physical life. If we are willing to make diet and exercise a priority so that we remain physically healthy for many years, isn't it wisdom to also have a healthy **spiritual diet** and exercise our **spiritual mind and bodies?**

My story of the young man has second miracle. He was set free again and is now a pastor with a beautiful wife and children. He is a **spiritual coach** in God's Kingdom!

Spend some time today asking God how **He** wants you to improve your **spiritual health**. Take notes. Begin to take steps toward **new life** and **health** that **fills** your spiritual life, leaving no room for unwelcome vagrants!

Some suggested reading: John 14-16, Philippians 3-4, Psalm 40

The Common Jesus   July 29

In the beginning was the Word, and the Word was with God, and the Word was God. [He] was in the beginning with God...
The Word became flesh, and lived among us.

John 1:1-2, 14 (WEB)

Jesus was a common name. It was like John or James. There would have been several boys named Jesus in Nazareth. Isaiah, the prophet, said that the Messiah would not be charismatic but common. Maybe Jesus had bad hair. Maybe He was even clumsy. We know He had calloused hands and dirty feet! And yet those hands brought healing and those feet received the loving tears of a forgiven woman and the nails of a sinful world.

I am common. I am Jesus' disciple. It is Jesus' plan to use me to show others His healing hands and forgiving heart. God had the eternal vision to come to earth – fully human – and show me The Way. Jesus had a frail human body that lost skin when He fell down. The sun burned His flesh. He was susceptible to fatigue and headaches. It may seem irreverent but Jesus was **totally** human! To see Jesus hitting His thumb with a hammer is to realize that He really **knows** what it means to have pain and **need** healing.

A disciple of Jesus is fully human. Jesus is my **only** standard and so I may not be self-righteous. I have only Jesus in me to **give** me righteousness. Just as Jesus was approachable and reachable because He was human, so God uses me to reach His hurting, lost children when I am **real** and **humble**. It has always been God's **only** plan to use His children to reach out to their siblings. It is our very weakness that allows His strength to flow to lift and heal His children.

In him was life, and the life was the light *of men. The light shines in the darkness, and the darkness has* not *overcome it.*

John 1:4-5 (WEB, my emphasis)

Remember how Jesus said that a person does not take a candle or a lamp and put it under a bowl but instead put it on a table so that it may give light to the whole room. (Matthew 5) Jesus wants His light in me to shine to the world. He wants me to be crystal clear so His light can shine unhindered.

My Keeper   July 30

But that you may know that the Son of Man has authority on earth to forgive sins" (he[Jesus] said to the paralyzed man), "I tell you, arise, and take up your cot, and go to your house." Immediately he rose up before them, and took up that which he was laying on, and departed to his house, glorifying God.

Luke 5:24-25 (WEB)

This is that great story about how four friends took their paralyzed buddy to Jesus because they heard that He might be able to heal him. They got to the house where Jesus was and it was so crowded, they couldn't get their friend and the mat on which they were carrying him close enough to Jesus – so they cut a hole in the roof and lowered the friend down! Now **that** is resourceful and desperate, isn't it?

The story is so familiar but once during the sermon for the children, a teacher asked the question: Why did Jesus tell the man to pick up his mat and take it with him when he left? The man was **healed,** what did he need a mat for? The teacher suggested that maybe Jesus wanted the man to use it...to bring someone else for healing. I imagine that the man had met a few other people in similar circumstances as he probably lay out by the city gate begging.

It's wonderful when God does something **awesome** in my life! And, yes, I praise Him and praise Him and praise Him! Wouldn't it be a great way to praise God if I brought a hurt friend to meet the One who healed me? As a nurse, I do not go to a new physician unless he/she comes recommended by someone else! And I do not recommend a physician unless I have known that MD for awhile and have a knowledge of his professional skill and his personal integrity. I highly recommend Jesus because I personally know His power and I know His love.

Amazement took hold on all, and they glorified God. They were filled with fear, saying, "We have seen strange things today."
Luke 5:26 (WEB)

They people who saw the man healed were "filled with "amazement". Now the awe could be 'wonder' but there also could be some 'fear' mixed in. People may see a change in me; a healing in my life and still be reluctant to believe and accept that it was Jesus who did those things in my life. Sometimes it is difficult to be joyful about a change in my life. Change **brings** change. It can mean changes in friends, priorities, schedules, and every aspect of my life. Bringing someone to know Jesus usually means building a relationship with that person and allowing them to see my life…as is, including the changes. It is allowing Jesus to shine through in my life so that another person will come closer…not just to me, but more importantly…come close to Jesus Christ. The chain of grace keeps going as they bring someone to Jesus. God's Kingdom grows.

Growing Up Like Jesus   July 31

It happened after three days they found him in the temple, sitting in the midst of the teachers, both listening to them, and asking them questions. All who heard him were amazed at his understanding

and his answers. When they saw him, they were astonished, and
his mother said to him, "Son, why have you treated us this way?
Behold, your father and I were anxiously looking for you."
He said to them, "Why were you looking for me? Didn't you know
that I must be in my Father's house?" They didn't understand the
saying which he spoke to them. And he went down with them,
and came to Nazareth. He was subject to them, and his mother
kept all these sayings in her heart. And Jesus increased in wisdom
and stature, and in favor with God and men.

Luke 2:46-52 (WEB)

I have found this passage to be troubling and not often used in sermons and Sunday School lessons. If the passage is used, we focus on Jesus' divinity and how He was teaching the elders at a young age, pointing out that his parents were clueless as to why He had stayed in the temple.

Jesus is said to be listening **and** asking questions. If you are a Bible teacher, that is what you want your students to do. Not that as a teacher I think I have all the answers but if the student is listening and questioning, he/she is learning and may find answers! 'Bumps on logs' do not learn. At best they can only regurgitate what is told to them!

Jesus' parents also discipline as I have. You question why the child would do something to cause you worry and fear. The first question should have been "What are you doing, Jesus?" to which He replied that He was about His Father's work. Later – a reminder to let His earthly parents know prior to His actions or send word as to what He was doing might be a better plan.

And so we then read that Jesus went home to be **obedient** and **grow physically – and** in wisdom. If I doubted that Jesus was **fully human** – Dr. Luke has set me to face the Truth. Jesus as 12 was still a boy. He was not ready to begin His ministry. I also must 'grow up' in my faith, learning to be obedient and learning God's wisdom.

Notice also that it does not say specifically that Jesus memorized books of the Torah or fasted three days a week or even attended synagogue every week. Luke may have assumed that we would all know that but maybe I am to learn through the way **God** desires to teach me instead of completing a checklist. God wants me to learn through my heart and make a life change. He **wants** me to grow into – an **alien** who is always longing for home!

First, I thank my God through Jesus Christ for all of you, that your faith is proclaimed throughout the whole world. For God is my witness, whom I serve in my spirit in the Good News of his Son, how unceasingly I make mention of you always in my prayers, requesting, if by any means now at last I may be prospered by the will of God to come to you. For I long to see you, that I may impart to you some spiritual gift, to the end that you may be established; that is, that I with you may be encouraged in you, each of us by the other's faith, both yours and mine.

Romans 1:8-12 (WEB)

Do you have **faith**? Do you have an allegiance to and belief in God?

I go to many baseball games and before each game there is the singing of our national anthem. Hundreds of people stand, put their hand over their heart, and look toward the flag that waves in the breeze, a symbol of our country and the beliefs that bring us together. Children still stand in classrooms and recite our country's "Pledge of Allegiance" that proclaims that **liberty and justice** is for **all**!

Faith is believing in something that you cannot see. You cannot give it a number or lay it out like a scientific fact. My husband does a lot of ministry with people who profess to be atheists and agnostics. No matter the specific issue that sparks the discussion of Scripture and ancient history, Henry will say, at some point, that belief in God is **always** going to involve a step of faith. There is no way to **prove** God.

Paul tells us that our faith is something to be "throughout the whole world". Certainly now, in the 21st century, the joy and hope of our faith is something to be shared! I meet people every day that have **no hope**. They are going through financial difficulties, children in crisis, marriages in crisis, and watch the evening news and they have **no hope** because they do not know Jesus and the Good News. That is where we are to share, tell, and live our faith out!

Paul says that by encouraging each other in our walk of faith, we give each other a gift of strength. Remember how John says that we will overcome by our testimony? When we come together and tell each other our stories of faith, we grow spiritually.

Yesterday I was looking at the weakness of my flesh, which brought me to thinking about how I can: Go into any book store today and find shelves upon shelves of self-help books that profess to be able to tell me how to pull myself out of any difficulty, turn my life around, and become **anything** I want to be. **I** can do it! Hogwash! I went through college on my own. I didn't count on God for anything. I drove myself through the next 20 years of my life and gave God only a once-a-week check-off, doing what was expected because some parenting books said it was a good idea to give my children a circle of 'good' friends that went to church. Yes, well that didn't work too well for me.

It was making a **decision** to take a step of **faith** and believe in Jesus Christ as Savior and Lord of my life that changed me and also changed my children. It was **faith** that brought my life to one of **hope** and **joy** that has nothing to do with circumstances but everything to do with **God's unconditional love.**

Always More of God   August 2

John answered them all, "I indeed baptize you with water, but he comes who is mightier than I, the latchet of whose sandals I am not worthy to loosen. He will baptize you in the Holy Spirit and fire,..."   *Luke 3:16 (WEB)*

John did something with water. Jesus did something with the heart. John did something in the physical. Jesus did something in the spiritual. Was John 'putting down' what he was doing? I don't think so. He was preaching the 'good news', the gospel, of repentance and exhorting the people to **turn** from their sin and walk a new life. He was speaking what the Spirit of God wanted to do! There is a **connection** on what happens on the outside and what **should** happen on the inside when I am baptized by water and Spirit!

If my spiritual life is **just** a checklist of 'stuff' that I **do**, then I will be sitting in a church for 50 years and still not know my need for a Savior! Too often we in the church look with our human eyes and decide our spiritual health (and the spiritual health of others!). Do I sing hymns in church or praise choruses? Do I raise my hands in worship or not? Do I speak in tongues or not? Do I put on my 'faith face' and breeze my way through life no matter what is going on or not? All of these external 'checks' have a spiritual counterpart that can only be 'checked' in truth by God.

Have I truly repented of my sins and made a change in my life? Do I have a personal, intimate relationship with God? Am I filled and empowered by God's Spirit to go through each day as He ordains? Do I present my worship of God from my heart no matter how loud or soft I sing? Do I care about the person next to me in worship? Have I asked God for a servant heart?

Jesus was about a heart change. So was John. Jesus showed us what a changed heart looks like. John said Jesus was **powerful** and would change people with His Spirit and with fire. Our old man is burned away when God's Spirit enters us. We are refined. When we follow Jesus' example through baptism, obedience to God, worship of the Father through our love and service to others, our heart can be changed. When our hearts are changed, we **want** to follow Jesus' example.

Let us open our hearts to God today. Let Him examine every corner of our lives. Let us be **completely** cleansed and **completely** His. Every day is a new day with God with opportunities for His Spirit to be **more** in us. There is **always more of God!**

Leaving the Comfort Zone   August 3

Now it happened, when all the people were baptized, Jesus also had been baptized, and was praying. The sky was opened, and the Holy Spirit descended in a bodily form as a dove on him; and a voice came out of the sky, saying "You are my beloved Son. In you I am well pleased."
Jesus himself, when he began to teach, was about thirty years old, being the son (as was supposed) of Joseph,...

Luke 3:21-23 (WEB)

Why did **Jesus** get baptized? I would think, primarily, to tell us to do it! I was baptized as an infant. For me, as a parent, dedicating a child is an important ceremony. When I was 40 and made my **commitment** to Jesus, I decided to be baptized just as Jesus was. The **ceremony** did not make me His disciple but it was an outward sign of the change in my heart. Even now, 15 years later – I can remember how **clean** I felt coming up out of that water! I felt like a child basking in her Father's unconditional love and approval.

Jesus was 30 years old, the son of Joseph, the carpenter. We are told nothing of His life after age 12 until this day when He began the ministry that He had come to do. What did Jesus do for those 18 years? We are told He was obedient to His parents and grew physically and in wisdom. For 18 years, Jesus, God-in-the-flesh, lived **totally** human. He went to school, did chores, worked with Joseph as a carpenter, and grew. He learned what it was to be a man and prepare to move on into His calling.

"Calling" and "ministry" sounds so holy and "church-y". Jesus had a passion in His heart – just like me. God has given me a call and He has given me gifts to equip me. As I have grown up and learned and watched for the opportunities that God places in my path, I leave the comfort of my home (comfort zone) and set out on the path He has for me. Jesus left His family and the carpentry to do what He had been called to do. When He was facing a crowd that wanted to stone Him, He did not turn back. When He faced Jerusalem, He did not turn back. Jesus and the Twelve and all His disciples since that time have taken the passion, the call given to them, and did not turn back.

Who shall separate us from the love of Christ? Could oppression, or anguish, or persecution, or famine, or nakedness, or peril, or sword? Even as it is written, "For your sake we are killed all day long. We were accounted as sheep for the slaughter." No, in all these things, we are more than conquerors through him who loved us. For I am persuaded, that neither death, nor life, nor angels, nor principalities, nor things present, nor things to come, nor powers, nor height, nor depth, nor any other created thing, will be able to separate us from the love of God, which is in Christ Jesus our Lord.

Romans 8:35-39 (WEB)

Listen to my Prayer   August 4

Listen to my prayer, God. Don't hide yourself from my supplication.
Attend to me, and answer me. I am restless in my complaint, and moan,
Because of the voice of the enemy, Because of the oppression of the wicked...
As for me, I will call on God. Yahweh will save me.

Evening, morning, and at noon, I will cry out in distress.
He will hear my voice...
Cast your burden on Yahweh, and he will sustain you.
He will never allow the righteous to be moved...but I will trust
in you.

Psalm 55:1-2, 16-17, 22, 23 (WEB)

Like so many of the psalms – this is a **great** one! Whether it was David or whoever, the writer is someone with whom I can relate.

I have a **relationship** with God. We talk all day. He is in my thoughts all day. Some might think that with that kind of ongoing conversations – I would have no reason to plead with God and consider that He might not hear me! I plead in our conversations because my mind allows thoughts that confuse and worry me!

Calling out to God is a **good choice**. Too often I find myself thinking of calling _____ (whoever). Now, God may tell me to call on my sister in Christ, but many times He would like me to get quiet and just allow **Him** to speak! God **will answer**!

One of the best 'habits' that I have cultivated is spending time each night as I lie down, turn off the light, and just talk to God about the day. I hold nothing back – good and bad. I repent as situations come to mind where I made a bad choice or said something I shouldn't or did something not pleasing to God. That makes for better sleeping! I praise God for the many blessings that He has given through the day. People He put in my path. The words of encouragement that He sent my way. The love I felt. The peace that **did** pass my ability to understand! And I give God all that … I don't know. I cast my cares on Him. I let go – so He can do! I claim His promises. It always amazes me how His Spirit will remind me of His promises. That will lead my mind to where I want to fall asleep – trusting God.

If I had to pick just **one thing** for which I am grateful to God – I would have to say that through all that He has brought me through – I have learned to trust Him. The refiner's fire of my divorce, my son's death, and all the 'little' things that I have had to let go (that I thought were so important!) – I have found – trusting God. That is such a precious gift!

Take some time today and read the whole of Psalm 55. Receive the fullness (the completeness) of God's words for today. And then when you lie down tonight, review the whole day and let God sift it out. Have a good night's sleep on God.

Temptation and the Tempter!   August 5

Jesus, full of the Holy Spirit, returned from the Jordan, and was led by the Spirit *into the wilderness   for forty days, being* tempted *by the devil. He ate nothing in those days. Afterward, when they were completed, he was hungry...*
When the devil had completed every temptation, he departed from *him* - until another time.

Luke 4:1-2, 13 (WEB, my emphasis)

Here is another Scripture that testifies to me that Jesus was **fully** human. He was **tempted**. Satan tempted Jesus through human frailties.

– "Are you hungry?" "Is there something you 'hunger' after?" Satan can subtly point you down a path to get it! Want a plasma TV but you really can't afford it? How about a payment plan or the 'lose your job coverage'?

– Want to be 'the best'? How much are you willing to pay in time and priorities to reach 'successful'? What standard are you using to define success and to whom are you comparing yourself? What are you making your #1 priority?

– Are you doing destructive things in your life or have friends with influence that are destructive? Will you throw yourself off the tower of stress, addiction, and bad choices in order to avoid discipline or achieve success?

The devil is a crafty, sneaky, and subtle **liar**! He uses my ego and pride against me like a well-sharpened knife! Look at Luke's words: he departed from him—**until another time.**

The devil will keep coming back and will turn away only when I order him to go with the power of Jesus and **choose** to stay as close to Jesus as I can get! Satan **hates** it when I worship Jesus!

Temptation and this world are synonymous. For now and until Jesus comes back, Satan owns this world – but he **doesn't** own me! My feet are planted on the Rock, Jesus Christ, and I choose to stand there!

> *Who shall separate us from the love of Christ? Could oppression, or anguish, or persecution, or famine, or nakedness, or peril, or sword? Even as it is written, "For your sake we are killed all day long. We were accounted as sheep for the slaughter." No, in all these things, we are more than conquerors through him who loved us. For I am persuaded, that neither death, nor life, nor angels, nor principalities, nor things present, nor things to come, nor powers, nor height, nor depth, nor any other created thing, will be able to separate us from the love of God, which is in Christ Jesus our Lord.*
>
> *Romans 8:35-39 (WEB)*

Messiah and Servant of All　　August 6

Jesus, knowing that the Father had given all things into his hands, and that he came forth from God, and was going to God, arose from supper, and laid aside his outer garments. He took a towel, and wrapped a towel around his waist. Then he poured water into the basin, and began to wash the disciples' feet, and to wipe them with the towel that was wrapped around him.

John 13:3-5 (WEB)

When I think of Jesus as a servant, this is the passage that comes to mind. God-in-the-flesh washing the dirty, stinky feet of these men. I would have reacted like Peter – hiding my feet under my coat and refusing to let my Teacher do such a thing! And then when Jesus explained that if He was not allowed to serve me in such a way that I could not spend eternity with him – "Well, Lord, just go ahead and bathe all of me!"

Everything Jesus did, however, was about serving the **common** people. He made a point to take those who were thought as "less than" and elevate them as worthy of His care.

He healed a widow's son. (Luke 7) He told a parable about a widow, using her as an example on how to pray persistently. (Luke 18) He acknowledge the unclean, sick woman and showed me not to be afraid to go after Him in my desperation. (Luke 8) And the sinful woman, (Luke 7) Jesus points to her, not in condemnation, but as my example on how to worship Him – giving all that I have and without embarrassment.

No one was too disgustingly sick (like lepers), too young (children), or too old (Peter's mother), to receive Jesus' compassionate loving attention or His gentle touch.

Whom shall I serve today?

Have this in your mind, which was also in Christ Jesus, who, existing in the form of God, didn't consider equality with God a thing to be grasped, but emptied himself, taking the form of a servant, being made in the likeness of men. And being found in human form, he humbled himself, becoming obedient to death, yes, the death of the cross. Therefore God also highly exalted him, and gave to him the name which is above every name; that at the name of Jesus every knee should bow, of those in heaven, those on earth, and those under the earth, and that every tongue should confess that Jesus Christ is Lord, to the glory of God the Father.

So then, my beloved, even as you have always obeyed, not only in my presence, but now much more in my absence, work out your own salvation with fear and trembling. For it is God who works in you both to will and to work, for his good pleasure. Do all things without murmurings and disputes, that you may become blameless and harmless, children of God without blemish in the midst of a crooked and perverse generation, among whom you are seen as lights in the world, holding up the word of life...

Philippians 2:5-16 (WEB)

Test: A Good Thing – Really!   August 7

[19]Don't quench the Spirit. [20]Don't despise prophecies. [21]Test all things, and hold what is good firmly. [22]Abstain from every form of evil.

1 Thessalonians 5:19-22 (HN)

Most of us have either been advised to test everything or we have advised someone else of the same thing. Testing is very important. There are many voices in the world that are asking for our attention. Who is speaking the truth? What should we do?

But the advice in this verse necessarily implies something else. It is this: Prepare to be tested! If everyone in the church is commanded to "test all things" then somewhere, sometime, you will come up to be tested. Then it is "crunch" time. We don't like to be tested.

This can be especially difficult for people who are in authority in the church. Generally pastors and teachers would like their congregation to test everything, but we're mostly thinking about the things other people say. We want church members to avoid the problems associated with TV preachers or the leaders of that heretical church down the road. We're less excited when someone questions us!

Jesus said, "Judge not that you be not judged" (Matthew 7:1). Some of us have grabbed that one and run with it. It's really a pretty good command. I have to say that, because Jesus said it! But I've learned something interesting about one liners, partially because I'm so good at inventing them. A one liner only works well when it is received positively and with good sense.

Let me give an example. On the cover of my book, *What's in a Version?*, I have the line **"the best Bible version is the one you read."** Now I'd still prefer that you not use The Living Bible (the old one, not the New Living Translation which is quite good) for serious Bible study. The translation is not adequate for that purpose. My point in that one liner is that the key issue in Bible translation is whether the people the translation was made from can read and understand it.

Frequently at shows or on the internet I have been confronted by people who explain to me that my one-liner is wrong. They point out examples of times when one could be reading a Bible that wasn't really the best.

Paul could be said to doing the same thing in 1 Corinthians 5 and 6, in which he tells the Corinthians to "clean out the old yeast" (5:7) and that we will judge the world (6:2) and angels (6:3). But is he? Of course not! Jesus himself, a few verses ahead tells us that we can know false prophets by their fruit (Matthew 7:15-20). If we are to know them by their fruit, we are going to have to look critically at that fruit. And need I mention the exception here, where many faithful servants of God have labored long and hard without any apparent fruit. Just consider the case of Jeremiah. The last story we have of him is of the people ignoring the word he brought from the Lord (Jeremiah 42-44). Jeremiah's preaching resume reads "ignored by every congregation to whom I preached." Today, of course, he's very fruitful. He's in the Bible. Who would have thought that in his lifetime?

There's something else we can get from Matthew 7:1, however. We must be prepared to receive the judgment we give. If I expect to test what everyone else says, I have to be ready to be tested on everything that I say.

Jesus calls us to be the church, the community of Jesus in the world. To do so, we have to be prepared both to hear and to speak. "Test all things" implies "be willing to be tested in all things."

In Weakness His Strength   August 8

Concerning this thing, I begged the Lord three times that it might depart from me. He has said to me, "My grace is sufficient for you, for my power is made perfect in weakness."
2 Corinthians 12:8-9 (WEB)

I read Henry's devotion from yesterday three times so far. It's one of those lessons that I really do not want to hear. I really do not want to learn. I would like to find a loophole in it!

I liked school. I still like to learn. I read for knowledge. I read for relaxation. I read to be challenged. I do not, however, like to be tested! I did not like tests in school. They cause stress even when I know the subject matter well. And so the message in Henry's devotion about 'testing' is not what I wanted to read. I want to find some **reason** to rebuke the testing! It is causing me worry and stress! This cannot be my loving Heavenly Father who is testing me!!!

After searching, I find myself reading Paul's words. Not even Paul could 'plead' and get God to remove his test. Paul says that the thorn was there to keep him from being too prideful. You could say that Paul's humility was **tested**! What did Paul learn through this testing? That God's grace was sufficient and that his joy, his success, -- everything that he really wanted – would come through **weakness** not his own strength!

I also am meditating on Henry's reference to Jeremiah. I thought it was a good point that Jeremiah did not grow any visible 'fruit' in his lifetime. However, I suspect God saw a lot of fruit in His son, Jeremiah, as he obediently kept speaking what God gave him…even when he did not want to say it! (those dead leaves around Jeremiah's Obedient Fruit are Whining Leaves!) Is it not a 'test' to stay faithful to God's call even when you do not see 'success' or 'prosperity'? Is the fruit that I sometimes do not see the fact that my relationship with God is growing and maturing? In a test, I can sometimes hear God more clearly because – hello! – I am **listening** more intently because I **want** to hear what God has to say! I want to know that I am not alone in the test! The Teacher is still in the room!!!

> *Most* gladly *therefore I will rather glory in my weaknesses, that the* power *of Christ may rest on me. Therefore I take pleasure in weaknesses, in injuries, in necessities, in persecutions, in distresses, for Christ's sake. For when I am weak, then am I strong.*
> *2 Corinthians 12:9-10 (WEB, emphasis mine)*

I hope that I will continue to grow and get to the place that Paul speaks. I know that God desires that I get there – because He is allowing the insults, hardships, persecutions, and difficulties!!! In those, I do **feel** the power of Jesus that gets me **through** that moment or that day. I just haven't found the 'delight' of those experiences!

God is the giver of love and peace. He is faithful to our relationship. He is sufficient for whatever may come in all my days.

In the beginning was the Word, and the Word was with God, and the Word was God. The same was in the beginning with God. All things were made through him. Without him was not anything made that has been made. In him was life, and the life was the light of men.

John 1:1-4 (WEB)

The **Word** is **Jesus**. He has always been. The **Word – Jesus** became **flesh** and lived **with** us. (v.14)   A concept that my limited mind can not understand: Jesus was **fully God and fully man**. Jesus was no less human than me. He was also God, Who had no beginning and will have no end.

John 2 tells the story of the wedding in Cana that Jesus attended with his new disciples. **Why?** Why did Jesus go to that wedding? Why do **you** go to a wedding?   Because you are **invited**! And **why** are you invited to a wedding? Because the people **like** you! (Unless you are a 'have to' relative!) Jesus must have been someone that others like to be around. They wanted Him at their home; at their celebrations.

Do you like Jesus? If you like Jesus, do you like hanging out with Him a lot? To get to know someone, I have to spend time with them. What would happen if I spent only 1 hour/week or 1 day/week or even less than 1 hour/day with someone? What if I spent that little bit of time with my husband? With my children? How would I know them? I want to be a disciple of Jesus. The first disciples spent 24/7 with Jesus for three years and **still** they did not understand Him! They expected the Messiah to come with **power** and restore the kingdom of God on earth! That was not Jesus' mission! Even a learned man like Paul writes like he expected Jesus to come back in his life time. Jesus did not.

When Henry does not react or answer me the way I expect him to answer – what is my response? Sulk. Ignore. Pull away. "You don't really love me!" "I must have done something wrong or you would have given me what I wanted!"

I do the same to Jesus. When the answer does not come or "no" comes instead of "yes" – I pull back. Will that get me an answer to the "Why did you do that, Jesus?" question?

In the story of the prodigal son, Luke 15, the father is watching, watching, always watching for the son to return home. The father **never** stops watching – because his love is never-ending. And then there is the other son who has done all that his father has ever asked – and that son also does not realize the love his father has for him. Jesus told that story because He wanted me to **get it** that He – God – loves **me**. Whether I am new in my relationship with Him and do not realize how much He loves or whether I have been walking with Him for 50 years – there will still be more love to realize! And as our relationship grows – so will my trust for Him grow.

Read John 1 and Luke 15. Spend time with our friend, Jesus, and begin to soak in the love that will grow the relationship. There is **always more!**

Overflow of My Heart   August 10

"You offspring of vipers, how can you, being evil, speak good things? For out of the abundance of the heart, the mouth speaks. 35The good man out of his good treasure brings out good things, and the evil man out of his evil treasure brings out evil things."
Matthew 12:34-35 (WEB)

Jesus was speaking to the Pharisees in this passage, making it easy for me to glance over it and dismiss it. He couldn't possibly have met these words for **me!** Let's check the dictionary to make sure!

69

'Evil'. Merriam-Webster's Dictionary (1997) says: "wicked, causing or threatening distress or harm".

My pastor posed some hard questions to all of us: "In what ways does my way of life hurt my family and friends?" Well, again, it would be easy for me to point to the difficulties of others that cause **their** families pain. It can be easy because I am not tempted in that way and so I can point away! But...I do have temptations and weaknesses that cause my family "distress" maybe even "harm". And so that brings me back to 'evil'.

Out of the overflow of my heart can come evil. It is the manifestation of that old saying, "Garbage in—garbage out!" If I allow garbage to come into my life, then there is every chance that something **smelly** will come out of my mouth! How does the garbage come in? Through my eyes, my ears, even my environment. With whom do spend time? How much of my time do I spend with God? How much of my time do I spend **listening** to God? How much of my time do I spend **looking** to God?

John Wesley, a great man of God, wrote his General Rules, which can be summed up in three points:

1) **Do no harm**. Wesley said this could be done when we turn away from evil of all kinds, especially those evils that are most often done over and over; even considered acceptable in our society.

2) **Do good**. Wesley said this could be done as we are showing mercy and doing good at every opportunity.

3) **Attending upon all the ordinances of God**. These are the spiritual 'exercises' if you will that will grow us in a healthy spiritual life like prayer, worship, communion, fasting, and reading God's Word. That is how to have a love-relationship with God.

My pastor has given me a lot of think about this week. As I consider the goodness of God may **that** be the overflow of my heart.

Life Choices   August 11

"You offspring of vipers, how can you, being evil, speak good things? For out of the abundance of the heart, the mouth speaks. 12:35 The good man out of his good treasure brings out good things, and the evil man out of his evil treasure* brings out evil things."

Matthew 12:34-35 (WEB)

What 'evils' are generally done in our society **and** hurt people in ways we are not aware?

I am going to warn you...put on some steel-toed boots. Your toes may get crunched!

What do you watch on TV? What books do you read? What magazines are in your living room or bedroom? Could you look Jesus in the eyes and answer the questions without looking away? I couldn't. Oh, I don't watch triple-x movies or read Jackie Collins novels or even Stephen King. But I do watch TV shows that are weakening to my spiritual health? I love CSI shows. Murder. Rape. Pedophiles. Reality can be horrific. I kid myself by saying that the 'bad guys' end up in jail or dead. And yet they are portrayed as people who have had bad or no choices that have brought them to this criminal end. What message am I sending to my children and grandchildren when they see me watching this? They believe that I approve of the content. **Hear me clearly**: I am not judging anyone else here but **me**.

What about 'trash talk'? Now ragging someone about who they are or what they have done has become a national past time! Professional athletes, movie stars, politicians all spend a lot of 'air time' cutting each other down, pointing out the flaws so that we don't notice **their** flaws! What message does 'trash talk' send to my children and grandchildren? That 'cutting someone down' is OK and even **fun** – unless you are the one being cut!

Jesus told His disciples (that includes **me**) that we are **not** to **belong** to the world. He has chosen us to come **out** of the world. (John 15:18-19) I am to be an **alien** of what the world sees has a 'normal' life. I am to be **different**. Can the world tell that I am different? Can my family tell that I live a **different** life? Do I walk my life in **Spirit** and in **Truth**??? What **flows** out of my heart, my life? Is it **healing** or **hurting** to the 'least', to the 'children' who are watching me? Jesus is watching and He knows.

I want my life to be so in love with God – that my life is about **passion for God**! Every moment of my life is about how I can turn the eyes of everyone I meet...toward God. I don't have to physically shout my faith but my faith in God **shouts** through the choices I make and the joy I know when I am walking in obedience to Him. May my heart be awakened to Jesus and His Way, His Truth, and His Life.

Who Will Be in Heaven?　　August 12

Behold, one came to him and said, "Good teacher, what good thing shall I do, that I may have eternal life?"

Matthew 19:16 (WEB)

I spent some time today chatting with a man who was very concerned about his father. "J" said that his father went to church all his life but "I'm not sure he really knows Jesus". Like many of us, "J" wanted his dad to profess his faith so that he, "J", would know that his dad will be going to heaven when he dies.

When I am looking for answers to questions I usually start in the gospels to say what Jesus says. In this passage of Matthew's gospel, Jesus tells the rich young man to "obey the commandments". (v. 17) When the young man said he had done all of that and wanted more assurance of his destination, Jesus told him to "sell everything and then follow me". (v. 21) Hmmm. Jesus did not say that the man had to make a 'public profession of faith', did He? Although if I obey God's commandments and follow Jesus, my life is a profession, isn't it?

"I think we will be more surprised by who **is** in heaven than who is **not** in heaven." – Henry Neufeld

> *For this is good and acceptable in the sight of God our Savior; who desires* all *people to be saved and come to full knowledge of the truth.*
>
> *1 Timothy 2:3-4 (WEB, my emphasis)*

When I am considering the salvation or spiritual health of someone, I believe that I first must remember that **Jesus** is the only one who will be judging who goes to heaven and who does not. But maybe I am not attempting to **judge** another – I am just **concerned** about them. Then here are some questions for me to ask **myself**:

– Am I living my life in Spirit and Truth?

– Am I who I profess to be to others? More importantly, does **Jesus** know my true profession or would He say He never knew me? (Matthew 7:23)

– Am I servant like Jesus? (Matthew 25:21-46)

If I answer those questions in the affirmative, then whoever has my concern will have known Jesus through me. It is the first, even **best** step, that I should take. Then, when the Holy Spirit gives the opportunity, sharing my experience with Jesus can be given to the person. Questions come. That is what Jesus did. He **proclaimed** the Good News as He **lived** the Good News.

Remember also Jesus' parable about the vineyard workers. (Matthew 20) Jesus told parables to teach. And I think a side benefit to His parables was to often 'poke' at religious leaders who thought they had all the answers. In this parable, Jesus reminds us all that whether we have worked in His Kingdom all our life or whether we said we work for the Kingdom on our deathbed – the reward is the same—**eternal life**. And as I consider this parable I come back again to the important point – it is not my job to judge and determine the rewards of others. It is the job of the One—**the One**—who is the owner of the vineyard!

So let us be about sharing the Good News of Jesus Christ – but make sure we are sharing it like Jesus did.

God's Good Infection   August 13

"You offspring of vipers, how can you, being evil, speak good things? For out of the abundance of the heart, the mouth speaks. [35]The good man out of his good treasure brings out good things, and the evil man out of his evil treasure brings out evil things."
Matthew 12:34-35 (WEB)

I have continued to meditate on my pastor's words and John Wesley's words. Remember the three rules for Christian living that Wesley listed?

1. **Do no harm.**

2. **Do good.**

3. **Attending upon all the ordinances of God.**

My pastor had some difficult questions for me also. Today I am looking at two more:

Am I seeking to bring God's goodness into everything I do? And is loving God a focus of my life? I am adding two others that have been on my heart today:

— Am I **allowing GOD'S** love to fill me?

— Do I **accept** His love?

I believe that I must **allow** and **accept** God's love into my own heart before I can **bring it** into the life of others and have it be a **focus** of my life. Remember the two greatest commandments that Jesus gave? Love God and love your neighbor **as yourself**? Too often I grab the "love God" and "love others" and forget or discount the last. Too often I allow the rewind button on the negative words spoken about me by people that I love to be played over and over. God wants to tell me the truth of **TOD**AY. God wants to show me where He has brought me—not rehash the mistakes of the past. Even Paul said that we can but **begin** to know how much God loves us. (Ephesians 3:14-21) But what a wonderful journey to receiving the love of God!

Worship is a wonderful way to **give** and **receive** God's love! As I speak/sing my love and thankfulness, praise Him for ALL that He is – He shows Himself. And where God is – there is His love!

Obedience is a wonderful way to **give** and **receive** God's love! As I walk/answer God's call, we are together and, again, where God is – there is His love!

Bringing God's **goodness** into all that I do means that I bring God's excellence, His virtue.

...seeing that his divine power has granted to us all *things that pertain to life and godliness, through the knowledge of him who called us by* his own glory and virtue; *by which he has granted to us his precious and exceedingly great promises; that through these*

you may become partakers of the divine nature, having escaped
from the corruption that is in the world by lust.

2 Peter 1:3-4 (WEB, my emphasis)

It feels like I have come full circle in my meditation. I started thinking about the 'evil' that I allow to creep into my life through my choices. God has given me **everything** that I need to escape the corruption or 'infection' of evil. God has given me **promises** and has saved me by **his goodness** and that 'goodness' is an infection that I want to catch and pass along to others. I want it to overflow out of my heart and be spoken out of my mouth!

Doing Well   August 14

For we hear of some who walk among you in rebellion, who don't
work at all, but are busybodies. Now those who are that way, we
command and exhort in the Lord Jesus Christ, that with quietness
they work, and eat their own bread.
But you, brothers, don't be weary in doing well.

2 Thessalonians 3:11-13 (WEB)

I once read a blog from a well-known Christian person who quoted part of this as a basis for not giving money to people who stand on corners with signs asking for money. The tone of the piece was very condemning and self-righteous. Again, I am taught a lesson about taking Scripture out of context.

When I read a verse of Scripture, if I am to truly begin to absorb the **truth** of what God is saying to me, I must read more than just A verse. It is more than the paragraph. It is more than the chapter. It is even more than the book that the verse is contained. History, culture, the author, and even my current situation all play a part in what God is saying to me in a given verse.

These verses are a disciplinary word to me about the times that I have been a **Christian busybody**! Discussing a person's prayer need and crossing the line into gossip when I asked for more information. I do not need details to pray! Paul says, "Jody, pay attention to what God is telling **you** to do – which does not include criticizing the spiritual lives of others!" Ouch.

"doing well" is doing what God wants me to do. It is walking obediently in what He wants me to do and think. It is walking my life in the footsteps of Jesus. Following His example. Grow weary in doing that? Absolutely.

Weariness may comes from 24/7 life that is in service, prayer, and personal study. It can easily become **un-balanced**. How many burned out ministers and missionaries do you know? Or people who were very involved in the work of the fellowship and then – resigned from every committee and even stopped coming to church. Burned out. Remember how many times we read in the gospels that Jesus went to the mountains or went apart from His disciples? Jesus knew He needed to regenerate and He did that. This weekend, I am going to regenerate. I am going to spend time with friends and recharge my spiritual batteries. With balance, I will continue "doing well"!

Kingdom work is the best work! It takes me into places I never dreamed of going! It brings me into network with people I do not believe I would have every met or had an opportunity to join in work. The work brings wonderful, usually unexpected moments when Jesus is present and blessings abound!

Let us in quietness seek Jesus' direction in our day. In humility let us obey His commands and serve without applause or fanfare. Let us follow Jesus' example of a balanced life so that we do not grow weary in doing good.

Leave It There by Rev. Dr. Charles A. Tindley
If the world from you withhold of its silver and its gold,
And you have to get along with meager fare,
Just remember, in His Word, how He feeds the little bird;
Take your burden to the Lord and leave it there.

Chorus:
Leave it there, leave it there,
Take your burden to the Lord and leave it there.
If you trust and never doubt, He will surely bring you out.
Take your burden to the Lord and leave it there.

If your body suffers pain and your health you can't regain,
And your soul is almost sinking in despair,
Jesus knows the pain you feel, He can save and He can heal;
Take your burden to the Lord and leave it there.

When your enemies assail and your heart begins to fail,
Don't forget that God in Heaven answers prayer;
He will make a way for you and will lead you safely through.
Take your burden to the Lord and leave it there.

When your youthful days are gone and old age is stealing on,
And your body bends beneath the weight of care;
He will never leave you then, He'll go with you to the end.
Take your burden to the Lord and leave it there.

I've been listening to this song almost every day on a CD. If
you are familiar with this hymn, the version I have been enjoying
may be – different. It is done with drums and electric keyboard
and guitars. The style of the hymn may have changed but I bet

that Rev. Tindley would approve if he saw how his inspired hymn continues to draw us closer to the Lord almost 100 years after he first heard it in his heart.

I decided to use this hymn for my devotion today because I do believe that God continues to give His inspired word to us today. How do I know? Because words like those found in this song, line up with the 66 books of Scripture that most of us know. God isn't silent. He loves us. When you love someone, you do want to speak to them!

So as you celebrate a Sabbath, allow the songs to speak to you just as Scripture speaks to you. Maybe even make a note of the songs that you sing so you can meditate on them through the week. You can find song lyrics on the internet. (www.google.com and put in the title in quotes) Allow God to continue to speak to you every day.

A Virtue – from God!   August 16

The Lord is not slow concerning his promise, as some count slowness; but is patient with us, not wishing that any *should perish, but that* all *should come to repentance.*
2 Peter 3:9 (WEB, my emphasis)

Too often I speak with someone (or look in my own mirror) and find that we are beating ourselves up because we are "not where we are supposed to be in our spiritual walk". When we make a decision to live as a disciple of Jesus, we become a "new creation", don't we? Does that mean the old person will never rear its ugly head? Does it mean I am always able to instantly resist any temptation?

When I brought home my children from the hospital after they were born they could not walk; they could not feed themselves. They could not read or speak in complete sentences. Someday they would be able to do that. It takes time to grow. I was not ashamed of them because they could not give a three-point speech on this, the occasion of their birth!

God is more patient with me than I am with myself. I allow frustration when I stumble to question my life with Christ and my ability to work in His Kingdom! If my old desires rear their nasty heads then I must not be His new creation! Ridiculous! Remember:

...he who began a good work in you will complete it until the day of Jesus Christ.

Philippians 1:6 (WEB)

In many ways, my growth as a child of God is like the growth I experienced in my early chronological years. In my new birth, God provides what I need to grow and "older" Christians do His work with me as they give the example, mentor, and pray for me. Just as I was patient with my newborn children and my teenagers, so God is patient with me.

There is one major difference in my two births. The first – I had no choice in being born. This time, I do. The power is God's. He puts forth all the effort. He provided the **perfect** atoning sacrifice; enduring all the pain. But the choice to again be born into a new **growing** creation – is mine.

So – I trust God. The more I stumble...the more I lean on Jesus. The more I press into His classroom of love and learning.

My Ministry   August 17

But you be sober in all things, suffer hardship, do the work of an evangelist, and fulfill your ministry.

2 Timothy 4:5 (WEB)

As ministers, we are all called to serve in God's Kingdom. God's Spirit has given each of us gifts that may be called 'talents' and it is in using these gifts that we are filled with joy and peace. No other time or place or person in our lives will give us that 'God-something' that fills the longing and we **know** that we are in the middle of God's plan for us. I have been thinking lately on some of the characteristics that describe this ministry that God has chosen for me.

Humility – from the moment I answer God's beckoning to 'come' and 'serve' using the gifts He has given me, I **know** that it is **all** about God and Him being glorified. If those I serve, see God more clearly and live their lives closer to Him – then I am on His path and plan.

Multiplication – My plans can **never** illustrate the magnitude of God's plans. In fact, I suspect that many times I am ignorant of how **huge** the plan is that I am a part. If I knew – I would certainly cancel the first characteristic of '**humility**'! God takes a mustard seed and grows it into a tree! He takes my 'little obedience' and makes it into a Kingdom Battle Won!

Priorities – God has given me His priorities: 1) Love Him 2) Love my neighbor 3) Love myself. God has given me a call and purpose for my life. In my case, it includes a family so He will provide the time for that also. He will show me the balance in serving Him does include serving Him **through** my family. If I am not pouring out His love on them but only on others, then I am not in His plan. When God gave me a family, He did not intend that I sacrifice them. He shows me how He does 'multiplication'!

Unity – Unity does not mean homogenizing. God calls us to **unity** as we worship and serve only Him. When we accept His perfect love as the perfect atonement of our sinful selves, we come together to make the Body of Jesus Christ. There is **much** we can agree upon and work together to build His

81

Kingdom. We can live in peace as brothers and sisters, uniting under His love and living as His children so that those who do **not** follow this Shepherd will envy us and want what we have.

I suspect that you have some characteristics of your own. Give it some thought. Maybe even write them down in the margin of this book. Come back to them in six months or a year and see what God says. Let us live a life of joyful duty to our Father that comes from love.

He has shown you, O man, what is good. What does Yahweh require of you, but to act justly,
to love mercy, and to walk humbly with your God?

Micah 6:8 (WEB)

My Prayer List   August 18

Trust in Yahweh with all your heart, and don't lean on your own understanding.
In all your ways acknowledge him, and he will make your paths straight.

Proverbs 3:5-6 (WEB)

I have a long list of prayer concerns these days. Those who are acutely ill, going through very difficult cancer treatment, having surgery, or are awaiting test results seem almost too numerous to count! I was just telling God that I feel "overwhelmed". And that is where I stopped. I was speaking to **God**. He does not get overwhelmed!

The first word of this very familiar Proverb passage is **trust**. To put my confidence in God is not an 'iffy' decision. Either I **trust God** or I do not. It is not a half-step measure. It is one side of the line or the other. If I **say** I trust God for these people that I lift in prayer and then **worry** – I am not trusting God for them! I am offering this person to God – and then I am taking them back again to carry on my own.

"What if God doesn't answer my prayer the way I expect? The way I ask?" Ah-ha! There is the real question. Do I trust God for whatever His plan may be? And if God is not going to do things the way I ask – then why ask in the beginning?

Prayer is conversation with God. It is speaking and listening. Someone that I love has a need. I ask God to meet that need. I ask God to heal that person. I believe and **know** that God **can** heal. That is what I ask and that is what I believe. I **trust** God with everything that I am! I do not **understand** all that God does and what it means. I just don't! **However**, I do believe that however the answer comes, God is the One who gives the answer. I know that how ever much I love that person that God loves them **more** so God's answer to my prayer will be the **best** answer for that person. The answer will be perfect because it came from God. It can be no other way.

My path is straight today because I am laying each burden down and put all my prayers, my hope, my confidence in my Lord and my God. There is no other that I would **entrust** with these very special people. I will not turn to the right or left but trust God for all!

Thank You, Lord! Thank you.

Minister in the Night   August 19

Look! Praise Yahweh, all you servants of Yahweh, who stand by night in Yahweh's house!

Lift up your hands in the sanctuary. Praise Yahweh!
May Yahweh bless you from Zion; even he who made heaven and earth.

Psalm 134 (WEB)

Do you know someone who ministers at night? I know a few that do that. They are those awesome warriors who watch and listen for God when many of us are 'busy with stuff' or we are 'sleeping'. It is not about a specific time of day that these warriors minister although I can think of two right now that **do** get up before daylight or stay up 'way past sundown and pray. And listen. And pray some more. And listen much, much more.

Jesus encouraged us to pray in our closets. (Matthew 6:6) He wanted us to focus on the One to Whom we speak and listen and not care about who watches us do it! I had a prayer closet once. Literally. It was under the stairs in our home. It was big enough for me to sit, not stand. I had some wonderful conversations with God in there.

God's house is where He lives. His sanctuary is a holy refuge where He lives and I can come. God's house has no doors or walls or windows. It is not decorated by specific, fancy furniture. It is where God **lives** and it should be with me at all times!

To 'minister' is to first serve God. I think that if I am not serving God then whatever I do for others will be...of little worth. So if I first seek God as I 'minister' then I will be on His plan and I will follow His lead! His Spirit will go before me and prepare the way.

To 'minister' is also to submit to God. Whether it is in prayer or doing a specific task, when I bow to God and know that He is the **all and all**; He gets **all** the glory! Have you ever tried to do something that you thought was a **great** idea? And it was! **But** it may not have been God's idea! OR I may have walked into all the light and grabbed the applause with all that I am — never turning to God.

The psalmist says to lift my hands and praise God! I can literally lift my hands all day and not give God any praise. It is not about where my hands are physically. It is where my heart is and the praise that comes from heart.

God will bless us from Zion. He will bless us from the Holy of Holies. He will bless us from heaven. I believe He blesses extravagantly those who minister by night. He, who never sleeps, (Psalm 121:4) sees the ministers who serve at night when others slumber – and He blesses extravagantly.

Let us give thanks.

Shine on, Lord   August 20

Seeing the multitudes, he went up onto the mountain. When he had sat down, his disciples came to him. He opened his mouth and taught them, saying,...

Matthew 5:1-2 (WEB)

When he came down from the mountain, great multitudes followed him.

Matthew 8:1 (WEB)

At that time, Jesus went on the Sabbath day through the grain fields.

Matthew 12:1 (WEB)

Crowds followed Jesus. Most of us attend churches who barely have enough people to fill half the chairs. Why?

Jesus spoke as one who had authority. He brought the Good News. Jesus' authority came from the Father. It did not come from a Board of men. It did not come from the hierarchy of the established church. He wanted to magnify and glorify the Father. His messages were also relevant to the people who were listening. His parables brought the people to a point of reference they understood and then blazed a path to where God wanted them to be. What are you being taught?

Jesus taught in the synagogues. Sometimes. Most of the time He was not in a church building. He met with the people wherever **they** were! On mountains. At the seashore. Where they work. In their homes. Jesus did not expect the people to wait on Him. Jesus came as servant and friend. He was approachable. He was touchable. Where do you minister? Who do you serve?

Jesus hung out with sinners. Jesus spent most of His time and invested Himself in 12 men who were – sinners! The men and women who spread the Good News of Jesus were **not perfect**! Jesus touched lepers. He comforted widows and orphans. He spoke **and did not judge prostitutes!** Is everyone welcome in your church? And if welcome initially are they encouraged and discipled – or just judged?

Jesus said He did not come to "abolish the law – but to fulfill it". Jesus did not come to throw out traditions but to clarify (?) what they were really all about. An author in our publishing company, Bob Makar, wrote a book, **The Messiah and His Kingdom to Come: A Biblical Road Map**, that is based on the principle that everything from the beginning has pointed to Jesus and the Cross. Traditions in and of themselves are nothing but dogma if they are not a Living and Active testimony to God's unending Love. Are your traditions inflexible and stale or flexible and fresh, meeting the needs of the people you serve?

The questions I have raised today are not easy but I hope I allow God to **be** God and that I have **no other** god before Him. I pray that if I am calling myself His ambassador – I am not misrepresenting Him!

Building My Faith Muscles   August 21

"...if you have faith as a grain of mustard seed, you will tell this mountain, 'Move from here to there,' and it will move; and nothing will be impossible for you."

Matthew 17:20 (WEB)

Have you ever seen a mustard seed. I have a small bottle of them in my cupboard. I used it in some recipe so long ago that if I needed mustard seeds again – I would go buy some fresh ones! The next time you go to the grocery store check out mustard seeds on the spice aisle. A mustard seed is about the size of the letter "o" in the current font print that I am using for this writing. Now consider that this is Jesus, God-in-the-flesh, saying that all I need is faith the size of this tiny seed. The seed is made more tiny when I think of its size in comparison to God's idea of size, being the Universe Maker that He is! Faith, tiny faith, in God and mountains will move. Just like that!

I met a man, Lou David Allen, this week through his blog, "What's a Snake doing in Paradise?". Mr. Allen said,

"We should have faith, enough to move a mountain, as Jesus said, but this faith is not for physical mountains, but spiritual ones." [1]

Mr. Allen nailed the difficulty in my faith. It is the mountain in my mind that seems too large for me to believe that it **can possibly** be moved. Jesus says that nothing will be impossible. Jesus speaks only the truth so where is the problem in my faith? In my head! How do you build a muscle? Exercise it! And so it is with faith. I must **exercise** my faith. Flex my faith all day and every day. There is no part of my day, no person that I meet, no situation that comes in my path that can not benefit from a flex of my faith. Think it! Speak it! Believe it!

A practical point to note: A journal or prayer notebook is part of the exercise equipment in my walk of faith. When my faith seems small or weak, jot down notes of what is on my heart. And watch God work! See how He molds me. See how He answers.

He set another parable before them, saying, "The Kingdom of Heaven is like a grain of mustard seed, which a man took, and sowed in his field; which indeed is smaller than all seeds. But when it is grown, it is greater than the herbs, and becomes a tree, so that the birds of the air come and lodge in its branches."

Matthew 13:31-32 (WEB)

And as faith grows it becomes great and big! Others may see the testimony of growing faith and find their own 'home' and place of refuge as they put their faith (even a mustard seed) in Jesus Christ.

1   http://thepracticalchristian.net/2009/08/whats-a-snake-doing-in-paradise/ (footnote checked 3/8/10)

Tearing and Trembling   August 22

Oh that you would tear the heavens, that you would come down, that the mountains might quake at your presence,...
But now, Yahweh, you are our Father; we are the clay, and you our potter; and we all are the work of your hand. Don't be furious, Yahweh, neither remember iniquity forever: see, look, we beg you, we are all your people.

Isaiah 64:1, 8-9 (WEB)

Yesterday was a good day and a difficult day. I woke up yesterday morning asking God to encourage me that day to stay the course that He has given me. He did that. **Big!** I praised Him throughout the day. It was good! No, it was great!

Then I went to a meeting ... and got caught in the church bureaucracy! Came out a bit battered and hurt! Had some quiet time in the car alone while Henry took a test...and God faithfully showed up through this chapter in Isaiah.

God **will** come in power and **"tear"** and cause some serious trembling! When God shows Himself, we rejoice with great joy as a child sees his loving Father. But if the child has been disobedient or rebellious, the joy may quickly turn to trembling as she awaits the consequences of her actions!

I want to be like clay in the hands of the potter as God molds and shapes me into the child He desires. Like a potter who sees the beauty inside the lump of clay and recognizes what **can be** long before **it is**! God sees me through the eyes of Jesus and comes closer. I fall to my knees asking forgiveness for my sins. God is gracious as He sifts through my heart and my actions…separating the sin from the obedience. When I ask, "Please, Father, forgive me and restore me!" He does. He wipes my slate clean and remembers my sin no more. The 'old Jody' is chiseled off like offending clay that is marring God's beautiful creation. God **does look** upon me and sees me as His child…truly loved.

And so I rested last night. **I rested with peace because of God.** I rested and healed because He is faithful and He will do it!

Take some time today to tell God exactly what you want. Pour out your heart to God and allow Him to give you the best of what He has in mind for you. Watch God come near with tearing and trembling!

He who dwells in the secret place of the Most High will rest in the shadow of the Almighty.

Psalm 91:1 (WEB)

Go ahead…read **all** of Psalm 91.

Political Words   August 23

Then [Jesus] said to them, "Give therefore to Caesar the things that are Caesar's, and to God the things that are God's."

Matthew 22:21 (WEB)

Politics has become an increasingly dirty business. Is it possible for a Christian to be in any way related to the methods or tactics of managing local, state, or national government without becoming soiled? If my email inbox is any indication, I would say "No"! Offering an opinion on a policy is "giving to Caesar". To attack a person personally, is "giving to me" instead of God.

> [Jesus said,] "For out of the abundance of the heart, the mouth speaks. The good man out of his good treasure brings out good things, and the evil man out of his evil treasure brings out evil things. I tell you that every idle word that men speak, they will give account of it in the day of judgment. For by your words you will be justified, and by your words you will be condemned."
>
> Matthew 12:34-37 (WEB, my emphasis)

How can I, as a disciple of Jesus, justify name-calling and snide jokes? How can I publicly call into question someone's relationship with God? Is Jesus not the Judge? I once heard a teacher suggest that on Judgment Day every word I had ever said or written would scroll across God's marquee for everyone in the cloud of witnesses to see. Just having those words illuminated and Jesus' eyes meet mine makes me hang my head and beg forgiveness today! What am I doing when I forward emails with a "This is good! Read this!" but speaking my agreement to everything that is written! Would it not be better time spent and operating with Holy Fear if I prayed for God's wisdom for us all? Do I trust the power of the Holy Spirit? I am not part of the silent majority! I am declaring my allegiance and belief in true power through Jesus Christ!

> I exhort therefore, first of all, that petitions, prayers, intercessions, and givings of thanks, be made for all men: for kings and all who are in high places; that we may lead a tranquil and quiet life in all godliness and reverence. For this is good and acceptable in the sight of God our Savior; who desires all people to be saved and come to full knowledge of the truth.
>
> 1 Timothy 2:1-4 (WEB, my emphasis)

Let us pray today with renewed fervor and confidence in the power of our Lord and Savior. Let us pray first for ourselves that we would be directed in our prayers in a way that pleases God. May we stand on His promises and believe in His power. And then let us pray for **ALL** in authority on both sides of the so-called political aisles that they may ask and receive the wisdom of God, speaking and acting in Holy Fear of the Only One to whom they must answer an account of their lives. To God be the Glory!

Death, You Lose! August 24

When I saw him, I fell at his feet like a dead man. He laid his right hand on me, saying, "Don't be afraid. I am the first and the last, and the Living one. I was dead, and behold, I am alive forevermore. Amen. I have the keys of Death and of Hades."
Revelation 1:17-18 (WEB)

God has blessed me by taking me through many "deaths" in my life. Yes, I do mean **blessed**. As a hospice nurse, I was honored to be in attendance as many people achieved victory over the disease that caused suffering. I saw the peace and joy come to their faces as they saw their Savior.

Looking Death in the face and knowing that you do so with the assurance of Jesus Christ is a glorious place to be. I do not fear flying in airplanes. I do not dread medical tests. I can only do it all because of the One who holds my hand – Jesus.

I used to have notes in envelopes addressed to each of my children and my husband. I would update them as milestones came in their lives and in my life. Now, embracing modern technology, I have notes on the hard drive of my computer. Jesus left notes for me that have spoken to me on good days and on my worse days. He is faithful to speak to my heart, day or night.

"Don't let your heart be troubled. Believe in God. Believe also in me. In my Father's house are many homes. If it weren't so, I would have told you. I am going to prepare a place for you. If I go and prepare a place for you, I will come again, and will receive you to myself; that where I am, you may be there also. Where I go, you know, and you know the way...

Behold, the time is coming, yes, and has now come, that you will be scattered, everyone to his own place, and you will leave me alone. Yet I am not alone, because the Father is with me. I have told you these things, that in me you may have peace. In the world you have oppression; but cheer up! I have overcome the world."

John 14:1-4, 16:32-33 (WEB)

Death comes with many faces. It can be the end of life here on this earth. It can be the end of a relationship. It can be the end of a 'season' in my life in which I will have to make some changes. It may be the death of an attitude or life style where I know I will (and must) make a change and never look back. The psalmist said that I would "walk through the valley of the shadow of death". (Psalm 23) I will walk **through**. I will not be setting up housekeeping and living in the valley. And I will **not** be walking through the valley alone! God is **with** me! No matter what name is on the death that I must walk through – God is **with** me.

Let us take a deep breath today and consider how death has been a part of our lives. And then let us read again Jesus' words in John's gospel and in Revelation. Dispel any lingering fears and walk forward with our hands clasped firmly and warmly in Jesus' hand. Live this life in joy and with the assurance of where we are going. Live this life with our focus on Kingdom work with the final celebration including **all who will come!**

First, I thank my God through Jesus Christ for all of you, that your faith is proclaimed throughout the whole world. For God is my witness, whom I serve in my spirit in the Good News of his Son, how unceasingly I make mention of you always in my prayers, requesting, if by any means now at last I may be prospered by the will of God to come to you. For I long to see you, that I may impart to you some spiritual gift, to the end that you may be established; that is, that I with you may be encouraged in you, each of us by the other's faith, both yours and mine.

Now I don't desire to have you unaware, brothers, that I often planned to come to you, and was hindered so far...

Romans 1:8-13 (WEB)

Do you know any missionaries? In my personal dictionary, a 'missionary' is someone who leaves their **home** and goes to live, work, and witness in another location. A missionary could be in the Appalachian Mountains or the inner city of Phoenix, AZ or in the Middle East, Africa, or Central America to name a few. God calls and people go. I hope you know some missionaries. They are a **blessing** in **your** life! Yes, the missionaries I know are a blessing to **me**.

I have been on six missionary trips. I was a team member on four and led two trips. It is an opportunity to **go** away from my home and be a servant and learn so much from those who are full-time missionaries, giving of themselves as they build relationships and bear witness to the Good News of Jesus in a very practical, day-to-day ways.

My in-laws are missionaries.   Even though (technically) retired, and Dad has gone on to meet Jesus, they are still missionaries. I do not believe you **retire** from your call. The most important life principle I have learned from missionaries is – you do not get to "pick" where you go, even where you live.

93

God opens doors; puts a love in your heart to serve a group of people and **you go**! Those who are willing have received amazing blessings by going ... many times without knowing!

Paul said that he had a **longing** to see these people and yet he "was hindered so far". Why would God prevent Paul (or me) from going to share His words with someone? **Timing!** The **message** may not be ready to speak to the heart. There may be **more** for the messenger to learn! The **heart(s)** may not be ready for the message. When revival came to Pensacola, I did not even know how hungry I was for God to speak so personally to me. Once I tasted His word, I did not let anything hinder me from going every night. I slept less – ate less-- but felt better and was better because I made God my #1 priority!

I am grateful that I am still learning about sacrifice and obedience. God has continued to send missionaries in my life to help me grow. I am in a season now where I am not **going** in the mission field. But I can still support missionaries with my prayers and offerings. I am humbled to be able to **serve them** in this way.

Change: Love it or Fight it   August 26

Therefore we don't faint, but though our outward man is decaying, yet our inward man is renewed day by day. For our light affliction, which is for the moment, *works for us more and more exceedingly an eternal weight of glory; while we don't look at the things which are seen, but at the things which are not seen. For the things which are seen are temporal,* [temporary] *but the things which are not seen are* eternal.
2 Corinthians 4:16-18 (WEB, my emphasis)

The older I get the more I have to work at being flexible and accept change. Change is a daily occurrence. Just as the stoplights change at every street corner so there are situations that come that require me to make a course correction. Is God behind them? Would God have me switch directions? Absolutely.

God took a shepherd called David and made him a king. He took persecutor named Paul and made him a disciple. He took a prostitute named Mary and made her an evangelist. He took a CPA I know named John and made him a pastor. He took a nurse named Jody and made her a teacher and author. Go figure!

The words that brought Paul to say "Therefore" at the beginning of our Scripture tell us about the treasure that we have in Jesus and that we are to testify/witness to His love and mercy. The treasure did not come to us without a price. Jesus paid that price in full. Our salvation is sealed. However, the path that takes us to that ultimate prize is a path through this world and it will include pain and suffering, just as Jesus suffered on His path to the cross. Our pain is **momentary** and if we follow Jesus' example we will keep our eyes on the **eternal** and choose not to allow ourselves be distracted or discouraged by what is **temporary**.

Fifteen years ago I had a dream and plan for my life. It involved many successes from this world. God wanted **more** for me. My mother said I was a "somewhat stubborn child". She was right. And the changes that have come in my life have come despite my efforts to try to jerk the 'steering wheel' from Jesus' hands. But Jesus' love is stronger and deeper than my will. He did not give up on me and now I find myself **rich** in so many ways that I could not have asked or imagined.

Change is still not an easy concept. There are only two options: **Love it or fight it!** I could not be described as **embracing** but I am looking with **expectation** on what is next! When I pray, I am learning not to be so narrow in listening for

God's answer. My heart is becoming tender like Samuel as I whisper, "Speak, Father, your child is listening!"

> *For all things are for your sakes, that the grace, being multiplied through the many, may cause the thanksgiving to abound to the glory of God.*
>
> *2 Corinthians 4:15 (WEB)*

'Out There' for the Gospel   August 27

Are you ashamed of the Gospel? Do not say "no" too quickly!

> *I am debtor* [I am obligated] *both to Greeks and to foreigners, both to the wise and to the foolish. So, as much as is in me, I am eager to preach the Good News to you also who are in Rome. For I am not ashamed of the Good News of Christ, for it is the power of God for salvation for everyone who believes; for the Jew first, and also for the Greek. For in it is revealed God's righteousness from faith to faith. As it is written, "But the righteous shall live by faith."*
>
> *Romans 1:14-17 (WEB, my notation)*

One night, I went to worship the Lord in a venue I had never been. I went to a "U2CHARIST". I watched young men and women put themselves "out there" to bring the Gospel of Jesus Christ in a forum that was intended – not for me who is already a disciple – as a lure to catch the fish that would not normally come. I am not a U2 fan. Except for a passing knowledge of one song that was featured in the movie, "Runaway Bride", I had never heard any of the songs. However, it took no stretch to read lyrics that directly point to Jesus Christ.

Paul said he was **obligated** to share the gospel with **all**. He made no distinction on the who and was willing to go **wherever** he was sent! Paul was an elitist before he met Jesus. He thought knowledge of God would come only to those who were good enough and chosen by God by their birthright and earthly blessings of wealth and status. Jesus corrected that by going to those who were **unclean** and **unwanted by those in the church**. Paul spoke his personal revelation with the words that all had fallen short of God's glory. And so Paul, Martin Luther, John Wesley, and those who follow Jesus put themselves **out there** with no safety net to draw **all** to Jesus Christ.

There will be criticism that is meant to wound, distract, and discourage those who are willing to present the Good News of Jesus Christ in a personal way, meeting people where they **are**. But for those who are willing to **go** where God opens the opportunities and learn to be "fishers of men" as Jesus teaches, the blessings of seeing the Light of the knowledge of Jesus come into a world of darkness is an experience not to be missed! Be Bold! Be Brave! Step out of your comfort zone and follow Jesus!

Riding in a storm today?   August 28

When he [Jesus] *got into a boat, his disciples followed him.* Behold, a violent storm *came up on the sea, so much that the boat was covered with the waves, but he was asleep.*
Matthew 8:23-24 (WEB, my emphasis)

He [Jesus] *said to them, "Why are you so afraid? How is it that you have no faith?"*
Mark 4:40 (WEB, my emphasis)

Being afraid they marveled, saying one to another, "Who is this, then, that he commands..."
Luke 8:25 (WEB, my emphasis)

Are you battling any fear? Job stability? Too much month for your present money? Are you on your knees every day crying out to God for your child? A loved one who is ill? Has cancer touched your family? Does someone you know have Swine Flu? Is someone you love currently in Afghanistan or in some other place defending freedom? The list is not complete, is it?

I hope you will take time today and read the three views from the gospels of this 'ride in the storm'. The story itself is not long but we need to read it. Matthew 8:23-27, Mark 4:35-41, Luke 8:22-25

Fear is a **virus** that infects each of us every day. Like a virus, fear does not look the same today as it did yesterday or last month or last year. It is always **mutating**; changing little characteristics to come **without warning** and take me out at the knees.

God is faithful. Jesus slept in the boat because He knew Who is **always keeping watch** and **never taken by surprise!** I have learned through divorce and death that God is always **before me** and has a hand already out to catch me when I stumble or trip. Before I know that I need a hand, He is there. Before I know I need to call out to Him, He is there to answer my call.

A fear or situation producing fear occurs – **"I trust You, Lord."** Quietly. Firmly. **"I trust you with _____."** State the person or situation. **"I trust You, Lord."** Recall the times – big and small, major and minor, that God was there **before** you. Remember the moments of peace in the middle of a storm. When everyone around you was upset, but there was a place of peace. No matter the squalls that blow – **"I trust You, Lord."** Remember that the One who calms your storms can do that because He **created** the wind and rain. He created your emotions. He placed that heart inside of you and can repair it when it is damaged.

Then they cry to Yahweh in their trouble, and he brings them out of their distress.

98

He makes the storm a calm, so that its waves are still.
Then they are glad because it is calm, so he brings them to
their desired haven.
Let them praise Yahweh for his loving kindness, for his
wonderful works for the children of men!
Let them exalt him also in the assembly of the people, and
praise him in the seat of the elders.

Psalm 107:28-32 (WEB)

Growing a Child   August 29

What makes a child go 'bad' or 'good'? First, let's keep the definitions of 'good' and 'bad' simple.

good – excellent, high moral life, superior,

bad - awful, horrific, shocking, poor moral life

Second, I am not setting myself as The Judge. I am also not claiming to have all the answers. My children are all grown now. I am **greatly blessed** that they love the Lord and are seeking to live their lives pleasing to Him. And I give **ALL** the glory to God for that. My devotion or time with you today is about what we can learn from God re: raising our children.

So, what's makes a child choose a poor moral path vs. a high moral path?

Moses exhorts us to teach God's laws to our children and their children. (Deuteronomy 4:9) We are not to just assume that our children will learn things if we send them to Sunday School. **We** are to teach them. We cannot teach what we do not know for ourselves. We can **tell** them but to **teach** means we have an understanding and knowledge of the subject. They **learn** and **believe** when they sense that **we** believe and **live** what we teach.

Proverbs says we are to **train** a child to go in Jesus' path.(Proverbs 22:6) If I may be so indelicate, it's like potty training. It takes more than one day to accomplish the goal and it takes repetitive encouragement and patience to get the child to **do** what you want him/her to do! The child will make mistakes and refuse to take time away from their play to go do the task and we as the parents have to stay with the plan and **train** them to do the 'right' task!

Proverbs also speaks about discipline. (Proverbs 22:15, 23:13, 29:15) The NIV and many other translations state discipline and include the word 'rod'. That brings up images of **abuse** when I read the verses and see a 'rod'. I believe there is a very clear line between discipline and abuse. I believe the line is defined by **anger**. When discipline comes from a parent and **anger** is the controlling emotion, not wisdom or love that a child would learn to avoid poor decisions, then **anger = abuse**. God wants to show us how to discipline. So when a child has brought up anger inside of us (pushed our buttons!), then let us take time and go to God. Tell the child, "I am angry right now and I need to go talk to God. Go to your room and I will call you back in a few minutes." How 'cool' is it to know that Mom and Dad talk to God? Seriously, taking time to calm down and ask God for His input and His wisdom is very good!

And then Paul gives us two words of what we should not do. We should not exasperate or embitter our children. (Ephesians 6:4, Colossians 3:21) We are not to make our children feel that they can never do good enough to gain our praise. Once again, we turn to God and see how He treats us, His children. God encourages us every day, doesn't He? But like our own children, we don't always hear Him! We need time with God every day to talk with Him and listen to Him. And so it is with our children. We can't encourage them in an off-hand way, as we are going out the door or as they fly out the door to the next event. We must spend time together and intentionally talk and listen to each other. Priorities! Discipline is important and we learn from our own experience—good and bad—what God must first correct in us before we correct our children.

When I was a child, I spoke as a child, I felt as a child, I thought as a child. Now that I have become a man, I have put away childish things.

1 Corinthians 13:11 (WEB)

It is important that we see in the midst of this love chapter that it is **love** that is the key ingredient to moving God's child from child to adult. Whether it is teaching, discipline, or training, it is **love** that brings up a child and keeps the child in the way that Jesus would have them to go.

New is a Good Word   August 30

[14]King Herod heard, because Jesus was becoming famous. Some were saying, "John the Baptist has been raised from the dead, and that's why these powers are working in him." [15]But others were saying, "It's Elijah!" and others were saying, "A prophet like one of the prophets." [16]But Herod said, "The one I beheaded, John, it's him, raised from the dead."

Mark 6:14-16 (HN)

When we see something new, we try to fit it into a familiar pattern. It's a normal human reaction. In fact, it's one of the ways in which we learn language. You see one tree, and you learn it's a tree. Over time, you see many trees, and you get an idea of the boundaries of the category tree. Some time later you might be traveling and see a tree fern. It would have many of the characteristics of a tree, but if you study deeper, you would find that it's not really a tree at all, that it's relatives in the plant family are somewhat more distant.

We carry that natural tendency into spiritual things. Whenever we see something happen, we want to put it into a category of things that we've seen before, that we understand. Why? It's comforting! People discuss labels a lot, and many are quite uncomfortable with them. Is someone conservative, moderate, liberal? Are they charismatic, pentecostal, or cessationist? We talk about the dangers of labels, and yet we continue to label people.

It's an ingrained habit. You've been doing it since before you can remember. It makes sense of the world. It allows you to deal with things that individually might be overwhelming.

The people of Galilee were putting Jesus into a comforting category. Did you notice Herod's response? He had every reason to hope that John the Baptist had not risen from the dead. He had killed John. But it's still easier for him to accept that John has come back from the dead than to look at the possibility that this is something new and different, something for which you just don't have a good category.

The people also want something comfortable and manageable. Oh, he's Elijah come back. That's pretty exciting, isn't it? But they were missing the possibility of something new. Others thought Jesus must be a prophet, like one of the other prophets. That's still a comfortable category.

But while all these people were doing the natural thing and fitting Jesus into a known category, they were missing the new thing that had come up. Their familiar categories that had made the world safe and manageable were keeping them from seeing what was really going on.

I'm not going to suggest you quit fitting things into categories. That's a basic function of thinking. But I am going to suggest being alert for new things, both physical and spiritual.

When a friend comes to you excited about a new experience, don't just say, "I've seen lots of things like that before." Consider the possibility that there's really something new. You'll encourage your friend, and you may just open yourself to a new experience.

When something new happens in your church, don't be too quick to fit it into the existing categories. Let it be what it is.

Look twice or three times to see what God is doing in that specific instance.

Don't be afraid of the new. Test, yes. But don't just test to see if it's familiar and reject it if it isn't. Test to see if it's God moving, and try to recognize something new.

Creator of All This   August 31

In the beginning God created the heavens and the earth. Now the earth was formless and empty. Darkness was on the surface of the deep. God's Spirit was hovering over the surface of the waters.

God said, "Let there be light," and there was light. God saw the light, and saw that it was good. God divided the light from the darkness. God called the light "day," and the darkness he called "night." There was evening and there was morning, one day.

God said, "Let there be an expanse in the middle of the waters, and let it divide the waters from the waters." God made the expanse, and divided the waters which were under the expanse from the waters which were above the expanse; and it was so. God called the expanse "sky." There was evening and there was morning, a second day.

God said, "Let the waters under the sky be gathered together to one place, and let the dry land appear"; and it was so. God called the dry land "earth," and the gathering together of the waters he called "seas." God saw that it was good.

Genesis 1:1-10 (WEB)

This is hurricane season here on the Gulf Coast again. Whether we have **only** a tropical storm dump several inches of rain or a full blown hurricane, there are no 'guarantees on exactly where the storm will go. We just know that it will go!

I remember the first time I saw the ocean. I remember the first time I saw Niagara Falls. I haven't seen the Grand Canyon – yet – or a whale splash off the coast of Alaska – but, Lord, willing, I will. Whether it is an expanse of ocean or the tiny details of a flower – I am **awed** by our Creator God. And God made it for me – for us. Do you accept that? God made it...for me. For you.

After creating us in His image, He gave us stewardship over the creatures and the vegetation. (Genesis 1:26-31) I noticed that this stewardship was not over wind and rain and the heavens. Hmmm. I would have to say that the recent events, including hurricanes, have made me more conscious of the need to be wiser in my stewardship. Instead of just **using** the creation, there is a good point to **use** but not **abuse**. Do I think about using recycled wood? Do I think about how I can make choices that will conserve gas; conserve energy. It is looking at God's creation and asking Him, "How do **You** want me to steward what You have given me, Lord"?

Through this season, I will be asking God for His mercy and grace over the many who may find themselves in harm's way. I will be asking God for His forgiveness of my – lackadaisical – ambivalent – attitude toward **all** that He has created. May my eyes be open to receive the beauty and wonder of His creation and be obedient in the way that I use what God has given me. May I take time to look at the birds of the air, the clouds in His blue sky, and His sunrises and sunsets that are so uniquely beautiful each and every day. How extravagant is the love of my Father!

Respectable Enough? September 1

He went out from there and came to his home country, and his disciples followed him. ²And when it was Sabbath, he began to preach in the synagogue, and many were amazed when they heard him. They said, "Where did this guy get these things, and what is this wisdom that has been given to him, and the these miracles that happen through his hands? ³Is this not the carpenter, the son of Mary and the brother of James and Justus and Jude and Simon? Are not his sisters here with us?" And they were offended by him. ⁴And Jesus said to them, "A prophet is not without honor except in his own country and among his relatives and in his household." ⁵And he wasn't able to perform any miracles except to place his hands on a few sick people and heal them. ⁶And he was amazed because of their unbelief. Then he traveled in the surrounding villages teaching.

Mark 6:1-6 (HN)

Do you have a really firm idea of how a respectable God will behave and who he can work with?

Think about it for a moment! It sounds odd when I put it so directly, but have you never wished that God would do things in a more respectable way? Have you never encountered someone else who thought that?

Korah, Dathan, and Abiram were offended that God had chosen one person to lead and one family to be priests (Numbers 16). God just wasn't respectable enough for them. A respectable God would have chosen pillars of the community, like them!

Balaam was offended that God spoke through his donkey (Numbers 22). A respectable God would have sent an angel that was visible to the human prophet.

The king of Israel was offended because Amos came from Judah, and wasn't trained as a prophet. A respectable God would have found a better person.

Jesus was born of a virgin, in a small town, to a relatively poor family, in Galilee, which just wasn't a respectable territory. Now we believe in the virgin birth, but imagine what the opponents of Jesus thought about it? Do you note that they mention his mother, his brothers, and even his sisters, but not his father? A respectable God would have made sure that Joseph and Mary were married before Jesus was conceived, even if it was going to be a virgin birth.

Jesus died on the cross. A respectable God would have arranged a better death, assuming he had to die at all. It just wasn't nice!

Is God respectable enough for you?

Will you listen if he talks to you through a child? Will you listen if his message comes through a homeless person? Can you still hear him if the music isn't up to your standards? Can you hear his voice if your pastor's grammar isn't perfect? Are you open to correction by the young person that you know has led a sinful life? Can you hear his voice through the mouth of another person in your church even if you changed their diapers when they were young?

Is God respectable enough for you?

The Work of Being A Disciple September 2

[10]When he was alone, those who were around him along with the twelve began to ask him about the parables. [11]And he told them, "The mystery of the kingdom of heaven is given to you, but to those on the outside everything comes in parables, [12]so that
They might look, but they won't see,
They might try to hear, but they won't comprehend,
Lest they should turn back to God, and he would forgive them."

¹³Then he said to them, "Do you not understand this parable? How can you understand all the parables?"
Mark 4:10-13 (TFBV)

We make a lot of assumptions about what Jesus would do or say about a particular situation, but one that I rarely hear is this: Jesus would like you to do some serious thinking and work it out for yourself.

Now I'm not telling you to abandon all of your principles and start from scratch, or to ignore God's clear revelation, but often things are not that clear.

Jesus often didn't answer the question that people asked. Do you remember the story of the Good Samaritan? You can find it in Luke 10:25-37. The lawyer asked Jesus how he could identify his neighbor. I suspect Jesus didn't think that was a very good question! The question Jesus actually answered was: Who behaves like a neighbor?

Do you hear some of Jesus' disappointment in Mark 4:13 when he asks, "Do you not understand this parable?" He has just told them that the mystery of the kingdom belongs to them. This is something they should be able to understand, yet he has to explain it to them. We modern students tend to go straight to the explanation that Jesus gave, but I don't think that was all that Jesus intended the disciples - or us - to do.

Verse 12 is troubling to many people. Why would Jesus intentionally talk to people in a way that they could not understand? Why would he not want to make the message clear? Surely if he just gave people all of the facts, they would understand and turn to the right.

But the problem with the disciples, with the larger audience, and with us is that Jesus has different goals than we do! We would like to get a list of the facts, so we could follow along easily. Jesus wants to transform our hearts so we'll be his type of people. We want the answers handed to us. Jesus wants us to learn how to understand the answers.

Jesus wants to change us into a different type of people: Kingdom people. To do that requires more than knowing stuff. It requires more than information. It requires commitment. It requires determination. It requires faithfulness. It requires action.

Jesus could tell you everything about tomorrow. He could provide you with the best answer to every question. He could keep you from having any moments of doubt and uncertainty. At the same time he would prevent you from ever becoming the joyful, committed, mature follower that he'd like you to be.

For those who are concerned with the last phrase of verse 12, "Lest they should turn back to God . . ." let me just say that I hear a bit of irony there. In Isaiah 6:9-10 from which Jesus is quoting, these verses tell us that God chose to speak to Israel through folks whose language they could not understand, because they had refused to understand when God spoke to them plainly. Sometimes the ways God chooses to use to communicate with us appear to actually offend and turn people away. Did God cause the fear of the Israelites when he commanded them not to touch the mountain (Exodus 19), and came down with thunder and lightning? Certainly, he brought out their fear. In that sense you could say that God made them afraid. But if God had chosen to come gently, the fear would still have been there and would never be overcome.

If Jesus had taught the crowds directly and plainly at all times, they might well of understood what he was saying, but would that have made them disciples? No! There is no shortcut to discipleship. Part of that process is getting the word inside you, welcoming it, and letting it grow, all of which takes time and effort.

A REAL Disciple of Jesus   September 3

Jesus said to him, "'You shall love the Lord your God with all your heart, with all your soul, and with all your mind.' This is the first and great commandment. A second likewise is this, 'You shall love your neighbor as yourself.'   The whole law and the prophets depend on these two commandments."

Matthew 22:37-40 (WEB)

They said therefore to him, "What must we do, that we may work the works of God?"
Jesus answered them, "This is the work of God, that you believe in him whom he has sent."

John 6:28-29 (WEB)

I was away from home most of Sunday and that away time included about seven hours in the car. I enjoy the time that my husband and I have in traveling like that because we have some wonderful conversations.

A subject very much in my heart is **discipleship**. After a person has heard the Good News of Jesus and has made the commitment to follow Jesus – what then? Or maybe they always knew about Jesus but there is a desire in their heart to learn more. In this time they may be looking for that peace that is beyond their understanding and the assurance and hope that can cover every aspect of their life.

I was discussing with Henry about the need for discipleship but what was in my heart was how Jesus connected with people without the requirement that they come to His classes cleaned up first! I would like to explore – for our thoughts (even discussion if you feel led to write me back!) – some of the people that Jesus met and forever changed! But what kind of change took place?

I wanted to start with the Scriptures from Matthew and John in which Jesus says that God's greatest commands were to love

Him, love my neighbor, and love myself. **Everything** else came after that. And He said that if I want to **do** God's work – believe in Jesus – all the other 'work' comes after that.

Give that some thought today and how those two statements from Jesus line up with your personal expectations of yourself to be Jesus' disciple **and** the expectations of those who are in your church or fellowship on what a **real** disciple of Jesus is.

Mary Magdalene, Disciple September 4

It happened soon afterwards, that he went about through cities and villages, preaching and bringing the good news of the Kingdom of God. With him were the twelve, and certain women who had been healed of evil spirits and infirmities: Mary who was called Magdalene, from whom seven demons had gone out; and Joanna, the wife of Chuzas, Herod's steward; Susanna; and many others; who served them from their possessions.

Luke 8:1-3 (WEB)

Mary, or Magdalene, is noted to be a "follower" or disciple of Jesus. She was a woman who had seven demons in her. Usually when we think of a person and demons occupying the same space, we see the actor, Linda Blair, in *The Exorcist*. If satan is the tempter, Mary could have also been like the sinful woman in Luke 7, a prostitute, or an adulterer, a liar, a gossip, a poppy (drug) addict. The tempter had acted, Magdalene had agreed, and her fate seemed sealed – until Jesus set her free!

Magdalene became a follower of Jesus. Though we are given information about who Mary **was** in the spiritual kingdom and who she **became** in God's Kingdom, we are not told that she started wearing only a demure, white robe and never again was permitted to stumble, less she be thrown out of the followers. We are not told how many hours of New Members' Classes were required before she was called a follower. We are not told

110

that Jesus permitted only **His** translation of the Torah to read, studied, and taught – and only by men!

Mary, called Magdalene, was a follower and **supporter** of Jesus' ministry because she came, began to work, and was accepted – **by Jesus!** Mary continued to serve Jesus even when she thought He was dead. (Luke 24:1-11) She went to the tomb, saw the angels, and heard the message from God. She was not believed. Her gender, even her former life, may have contributed to that disbelief.

We do not know any more about Mary from Scripture. Historical data lends no more clear information. Magdalene was a follower of Jesus Christ. Jesus set her free out of His great love, while she was yet a sinner! She was never the same. And so she **served** Jesus probably imperfectly. She may be called "a saint" just as I am (Revelation 19:8) – by the grace of God.

Do you see yourselves and others as God's saints or is it a small, exclusive group?

Samaritan Woman, Disciple September 5

> *He needed to pass through Samaria. So he came to a city of Samaria, called Sychar, near the parcel of ground that Jacob gave to his son, Joseph. Jacob's well was there. Jesus therefore, being tired from his journey, sat down by the well. It was about the sixth hour. A woman of Samaria came to draw water.*
>
> *John 4:4-7 (WEB)*

Jesus has a conversation with a Samaritan woman. Comparing it to His day and culture, that would be like a famous Christian minister having a conversation with a well-known prostitute in board daylight at a local gas station. It would not have been a secret!

Jesus tells the woman that He has a way for her to never be humiliated (thirsty) again but first He establishes His "rep".

111

Jesus tells her that He knows things about her (and yet still spoke to her with respect). Jesus also spoke prophetically, telling her that **all** (Jew and Samaritan) will worship God in a new and different way.

Jesus went out of His way to go where He would not be welcomed or even liked. He sought this woman to bring her words of eternal life – but also to "birth" an evangelist who would tell many and bring them to the Word. (John 4:39-42) Jesus gave His **personal** approval to a **woman** who was also hated by church leaders and church goers alike.

By the standards of many denominations and non-denominations fellowships, Jesus chose one who would never be chosen by the synagogue's deacon board; never be accepted to a seminary. Jesus chose the one with an empathetic heart who answered **His** call.

Does your fellowship encourage, empower, and listen to those who are called and anointed by God or **only** those with seminary and graduate credentials?

Skye McCracken, from western Kentucky, in his *Kyrie Eleison* blogpost offers some pastoral thoughts on the subject.[1]

1   http://revdsky.blogspot.com/2009/08/do-we-need-to-reconsider-seminary.html (link checked 3/8/10)

The Rich Young Man — Not! September 6

Behold, [man] came to him and said, "Good teacher, what good thing shall I do, that I may have eternal life?"

Matthew 19:16 (WEB)

The rich young man thought he had it all – except that **assurance** of what was next after this life. He had all that money could buy **and** was a **good** man! He obeyed God's commandments. He knew those commands so we can surmise that he was educated in the Torah, probably attended synagogue regularly.

Too many of us fall into the deception that if we attend church and know Scripture we are disciples of Jesus. Our actions can be checked off on the approved list but our hearts are **not totally sold out** to Jesus.

"...I, Yahweh your God, am a jealous God..."

Exodus 20:5 (WEB)

What do we think this means? Can we bargain with God about our priorities? Who do I love more – God or the things and priorities of **this** world? What is the truth hidden in my heart? Who or what do I love the best?

Jesus told the man that it was not **lack** that would keep him from eternal life but his desire for wealth and achievement over desire to be obedient to God. The man went away sad and unfulfilled because he could not give away all that **he** had done and do what **God** wanted him to do.

How much do I limit God or what I will hear as an answer from God when I ask Him a question? Am I willing to **give all** to **receive more?**

Disciple: Imperfect but His September 7

For this, I was appointed as a preacher, an apostle, and a teacher of the Gentiles. For this cause I also suffer these things. Yet I am not ashamed, for I know him whom I have believed, and I am persuaded that he is able to guard that which I have committed to him against that day.

2 Timothy 1:11-12 (WEB)

And so after spending the week studying the disciples of Jesus and meditating on what their examples and Jesus' words mean in my life, I have come to treasure some truths in my heart.

- Most of the disciples had little in the way of worldly wealth. Those that did they seem to be giving to those who did not and supporting ministries (Acts 6, Philippians 4).

- All were out of their "comfort zone". Fishermen like Peter found themselves speaking to educated church leaders. Elite church leaders, like Paul, were speaking to common people, non-Jews (Gentiles). I didn't find any who had family and friends who listened to them or went out of their way to support them. Strangers did that! Jesus said that those who were doing God's will were **His** family. (Matthew 12:48-50) and that no prophet was welcome at home (Luke 4:24).

- Out of their comfort zones, disciples learned to be totally dependent upon God for their needs, whether that was food, their health and safety, helpers in ministry, even where to spread His Good News. Paul said he had learned to "be content in all things" (Philippians 4:11) and yet his many words tell me that he believed and spoke in faith what he **wanted** to walk in his life.

- Making a mistake, even a whopper, does not mean Jesus will cross you off the assignment list. Peter gives his life's testimony when he denied Jesus x 3 then is reinstated x 3 ("Do you love me?"). (John 21:15-23) Jesus did not pick perfect people but sinners. He wanted **sinners** to share with **sinners** that there is hope in Him.

- Some of us are "Martha's", ready to **do** any task we see that needs doing! Some of us are "Mary's" soaking up the words of God, worshiping at His feet, and receiving His unearned love and forgiveness. We are comfortable in those roles. Jesus wants me to be balanced in both and leads me into different seasons so I can grow in both. If

114

I do not **learn** in <u>**both**</u> seasons—I may find myself stuck, locked in, or otherwise **detained** until I learn what Jesus desires me to have.

Being a disciple is about mountaintop experiences (Mark 9) and crucifixions. (Luke 9:23) Paul said it most eloquently and truly in our verses today. I am not ashamed to be a disciple nor of the news that He has given me to share. All that I am, all that I do, I give it to Jesus for Him to sift, keeping what is good in His eyes and forgiving what is not – until we meet face to face: King of Kings and disciple.

Shout to God   September 8

So the people shouted, and the priests blew the trumpets. It happened, when the people heard the sound of the trumpet, that the people shouted with a great shout, and the wall fell down flat, so that the people went up into the city, every man straight before him, and they took the city.

Joshua 6:20 (WEB)

There have been times that I pray and pray and pray about a situation or for a specific person and time seems to drag on and on and I wonder if God is going to answer. Then I remember how faithful God is and I know that He **will** answer, but when???

Peter tells me that God isn't slow but His timing is not like how I think of time. I get that. God is about eternity so what does one hour or one day mean?

I read a word from J. Lee Grady who writes for Charisma magazine. I hope you will take time today to go to this link[1] and read what he has to say about shouting to God. Some of you may have never raised your voice to God. Maybe you think that isn't something that you should do and you wouldn't think about doing it much less actually do it! I hope you have never had anything happen in your life that warrants shouting at God. I have. I can promise you that you can shout at God – and live to tell the story.

Shouting isn't about volume as in decibels but it is about the volume of your desperation. The stories of volume that I read in Scripture seem to agree with that. So back to my first paragraph – I am praying. I am believing that God is faithful. Am I desperate? Because when I am desperate I know that God is power and love and trustworthy. Yup, worthy of my trust. I am **shouting** what I know and believe.

Go now and read Grady's words. Then get quiet with God – let the shouting begin!

---

1   http://www.charismamag.com/index.php/fire-in-my-bones/23119-put-some-punctuation-in-your-praise (checked on 3/8/10)

Forgiveness Today   September 9

[Jesus said,] "For if you forgive men their trespasses, your heavenly Father will also forgive you. 6:15 But if you don't forgive men their trespasses, neither will your Father forgive your trespasses."
Matthew 6:14-15 (WEB)

"Forgiveness" is a grown-up Christian concept. It is one of the points that my pastor has brought before me. He has been **strongly** preaching and exhorting us to "GROW UP!" and one of those ways is to deal with Jesus' words from Matthew 18:15-17. If a brother or sister sins against me, then talk to him/her about it. If the person does not acknowledge the sin, then take another sister/brother and go to them as a witness. If that doesn't work – bring it to the church. If that doesn't work, treat him as a pagan. Sounds pretty harsh! Let's look at this a step at a time.

How does another Christian 'sin' against you? Anybody every lied or gossiped about you? Anyone used their influence to prevent you from doing your job? Answering your call? Ouch. I bet some memory has come to mind!

Next comes the resolution part. That's difficult. In Matthew 6 Jesus says we are to forgive if we desire to be forgiven. I certainly have plenty that needs forgiveness! Jesus said in Matthew 17 that if someone sins I should help them to come back to the path of forgiveness! BUT – and that's a key part – the person may not want to acknowledge their sin and so not 'need' the forgiveness. Where does that leave me and forgiveness?

On that Sunday morning, as my pastor spoke, I immediately had the image of someone who has recently sinned against me. Yes, this person had sinned. My husband could testify to the fact. However, as I bowed my head and knew that the Holy Spirit was asking me to extend forgiveness to this person I also knew that this person did not see their act as a sin. That lack of knowledge on their part did not preclude me from being obedient and, from my heart, give the forgiveness. Now I don't know all that happened at that moment. I am, after all, not able to understand all that is God. I just know that a 'heaviness' that has weighed me down for some weeks – left me. I walked out of that service lighter and whole in my spirit. As for the rest of the reconciliation, that is for God to direct. I have not felt God's direction to go to this person yet. I do not have peace about doing that. So I will wait and pray.

Forgiveness is a powerful weapon against satan who prowls about. Forgiveness is birthed from love. God's love. The 'bad guys' of this world hate that! It comes forth through no power of my own, just a choice to allow **God** to work within me.

If during this devotion, an image comes; a need to forgive, do not let the moment past. Allow God to speak to you and tell you **His** next step. Follow Him. You will be glad you did!

I will give thanks to Yahweh with my whole heart. I will tell of all your marvelous works.
I will be glad and rejoice in you. I will sing praise to your name, O Most High...
Those who know your name will put their trust in you, for you, Yahweh, have not forsaken those who seek you.
Sing praises to Yahweh, who dwells in Zion, and declare among the people what he has done.

Psalm 9:1-2, 10-11 (WEB)

The other day I was thinking about shouting. Today I am thinking about responses. I am thankful today. As I spent some time with God yesterday I again knew:

— God was already there, waiting for me. I did not have to get His attention. God was there. His attention was not distracted. He made me feel like I was His only conference in the day. Yeah! Right!

— God let me talk and talk and talk. I could be 'chatty' or as 'closed-mouth' as I wanted. God did not cut me off and He did not have to pry it out of me. He already knew. My talking helps **me** as I unload and allow the verbalizing of my thoughts to sift the emotion. As I say some things – I think, "Duh!" and see so much more clearly. God is Light and He illuminates, driving out the confusion and half-truths that are **not** Him.

— As I wind down, I hear God's voice much more clearly. Getting my shadows and blankets of "stuff" out of the way enables my human ears to hear what God has to say. To make prayer only about me and what I want to tell God is like never allowing my husband to speak and expecting our marriage to flourish! Being quiet before

God is the **gold** in my prayer time as I sit and do not hurry the silence.

- Ending prayer and ending my day with thanksgiving for all that God has done is a way to rest so good in the presence of God. Going to sleep thanking God or counting my many blessings, is better than any fancy bed and certainly the sweetest music to my spirit.

Whether you begin your day with the Lord or end your day with the Lord or just walk through the entire day just having conversations with your God – there is always a piece to add or 'flex' a bit for God to have a fresh time with you. Whatever it is that God has suggested to you – try it! You will like it!!

May the words of my mouth and the meditation of my heart be pleasing in your sight, O LORD, my Rock and my Redeemer.

Psalm 19:14 (NIV)

Pray for our Nation   September 11

"If I shut up the sky so that there is no rain, or if I command the locust to devour the land, or if I send pestilence among my people; if my people, who are called by my name, shall humble themselves, and pray, and seek my face, and turn from their wicked ways; then will I hear from heaven, and will forgive their sin, and will heal their land. Now my eyes shall be open, and my ears attentive, to the prayer that is made in this place."

2 Chronicles 7:13-15 (WEB)

There are many prayer meetings going on today, the anniversary of 9/11 tragedies of 2001. Christians come together to pray for our country and leaders. I do a happy dance in my office to think of so many praying. However, websites tell me that there are some **un-Godly** prayers that will be offered.

119

Many are encouraging groups to pray for the downfall of the current presidential administration. Even the death of the president. Oh, my brothers and sisters, grab on to some **Holy Fear** and examine your hearts! Dr. Allan Bevere, Methodist pastor and author, said in his recent blog "I am sorry, the political platform of the DNC and the RNC are not the equivalents to the Sermon on the Mount, and if you think they are even close, you need to be introduced anew to the biblical narrative."[1]

To pray for someone is to lift them before God. It is to ask God to come into their lives. Come closer. To bless someone with all that God is. Does the Bible reflect prayers where someone asks God to curse another? Yes. There are numerous places in the Old Testament where enemies of Israel are cursed by those crying out to God from their oppression and exile. **What did Jesus say?**

> *"You have heard that it was said, 'You shall love your neighbor, and hate your enemy. But I tell you, love your enemies, bless those who curse you, do good to those who hate you, and pray for those who mistreat you and persecute you, that you may be children of your Father who is in heaven. For he makes his sun to rise on the evil and the good, and sends rain on the just and the unjust. For if you love those who love you, what reward do you have? Don't even the tax collectors do the same? If you only greet your friends, what more do you do than others? Don't even the tax collectors* [and politicians!] *do the same? Therefore you shall be perfect, just as your Father in heaven is perfect."*
>
> Matthew 5:43-48 *(WEB, my addition)*

Let us pray today for our nation and our leaders. Let us pray with renewed fervor for God's wisdom which He said He would give freely if we ask. Let us pray for God's presence in meetings that it be His voice that is heard with the respect and humility that pervades all who are present. May individuals hear the call of God in their lives causing them to lay down political agendas and take up instead the cross they have been asked to carry.

"May the words of my mouth and the meditations of my heart be pleasing to You this day, O Lord"

Psalm 19:14 (my paraphrasing)

---

1   http://arbevere.blogspot.com/2009/09/i-done-with-health-care.html

I am Dirt in God's Hands   September 12

The word which came to Jeremiah from Yahweh, saying, Arise, and go down to the potter's house, and there I will cause you to hear my words. Then I went down to the potter's house, and behold, he was making a work on the wheels. When the vessel that he made of the clay was marred in the hand of the potter, he made it again another vessel, as seemed good to the potter *to make it.*

Jeremiah 18:1-4 (WEB, my emphasis)

As he passed by, he saw a man blind from birth. His disciples asked him, "Rabbi, who sinned, this man or his parents, that he was born blind?"

Jesus answered, "Neither did this man sin, nor his parents; but, that the works of God might be revealed in him. I must work the works of him who sent me, while it is day. The night is coming, when no one can work. While I am in the world, I am the light of the world." When he had said this, he spat on the ground, made mud with the saliva, anointed the blind man's eyes with the mud,..

John 9:1-6 (WEB)

As I have been meditating on God's words this week about prayer – it is no coincidence as I am walking through a difficult season in my personal life. And so God, who is faithful, and loves me so much, brings me to these verses today. He asks me

121

a question: "Will you be the dirt that I use, Jody?" Oh my goodness! And here I was expecting Jesus to ask me to be His well-known, white-robed disciple!

God speaks to His prophet, Jeremiah, in this passage, several years after Jeremiah began speaking God's words. Jeremiah had already been through "some stuff". To me, God is reminding Jeremiah (and **me**) that **He** is the potter who takes the wet, common clay and **molds** and **presses** the clay into something **useful** and **beautiful**. The clay becomes useful and beautiful because of the hands of the One who does not give up on clay that may be less than perfect and less than malleable in and of itself.

Jesus comes to **fulfill** what was begun in the Old Testament. Jesus takes dirt; adds His own spit (something of Himself) and dirt goes from **just being** dirt – to being an instrument of healing. WOW! Dirt is not just something to be walked on or made into bricks. It is a wondrous tool in the Hand of God!

Am I willing to be just dirt? Am I willing to be nothing of consequence by the world's standards? Am I willing **to be** – in God's hands? Am I willing **to be** – whatever, whenever, wherever, and to whomever God decides me to be? I have the choice and it involves more than saying, "Here I am, Lord!" It is also a choice of where my eyes are turned. It is a choice of how my heart is open for Jesus' direction or my desires.

> Have Thine own way, Lord! Have Thine own way!
> Thou art the potter, I am the clay; Mold me and make me after Thy will,
> While I am waiting yielded and still.
> Have Thine own way, Lord! Have Thine own way!
> Hold o'er my being absolute sway! Fill with Thy Spirit till all shall see
> Christ only, always, living in me.
> *Adelaide Pollard, 1907*

But now in Christ Jesus you who once were far away have been brought near through the blood of Christ.

Ephesians 2:13 (NIV)

I hope that everyone who is reading this has seen *The Passion of the Christ* movie. My son, James, bought that DVD near the end of his life so I actually have it in my movie library. As I watched the movie in the theater the first time (with my box of Kleenex) I was pierced through the heart with the knowledge, even as a glimpse, of how much God loves me. I said to my husband that night, "I do not need to see that movie again. Once was enough." I was right and wrong. I have not watched the movie again. I have needed to recall some vivid scenes. I have needed to remember how much God loves me. I **am** bought near by the blood of the Messiah.

The atonement – the reconciliation – of God to His children was not achieved by some **clean, sterile, and emotionless ritual**. The atonement was **messy** by physical standards. It was **emotional**—filled with emotion even!   It was about **love**—extravagant, no-holding-back **love**! It was the Messiah, the Savior, giving **all** that He had, physically and emotionally, to rescue and restore the one of His heart!

Here is one of those God Mysteries I cannot comprehend: Jesus died – was the atoning sacrifice of all mankind. He did it **once** for **all**. But – Jesus also went to the cross, took the lashes, carried the cross and then laid down on it, was nailed to it, hung there, gave His last drop of blood with His eyes … on me. God-in-the-flesh, Jesus, sees the <u>all</u> – and sees me. **The Passion of the Christ**, Jesus' love for _____. (Go ahead. Put your name there. It is the truth.)

As they were eating, Jesus took bread, gave thanks for it, and broke it. He gave to the disciples, and said, "Take, eat; this is my body." 26:27 He took the cup, gave thanks, and gave to them, saying, "All of you drink it, 26:28 for this is my blood of the new covenant, which is poured out for many for the remission of sins. 26:29 But I tell you that I will not drink of this fruit of the vine from now on, until that day when I drink it anew with you in my Father's Kingdom."

Matthew 26:26-29 (WEB)

From Adam, we have chosen sin over God. Sin separates us from a holy and sinless God. He cannot remain holy, He cannot remain just and let us 'off the hook'. There had to be an innocent volunteer that would die physically and spiritually to take man's judgment. Only God's Son, God-in-the-flesh, would be perfect enough. The rest of us have "sinned and fallen short."

Jesus is not **a** son but **the** Son of God. Jesus had no beginning just as God had no beginning. It is one of those mysteries that my finite mind cannot wrap itself around: Three Person in One God. Jesus came in total humility. Born in a stable, raised in a village of no account, and surrounding Himself with uneducated, poor disciples, Jesus came – to die. satan trembled that night in Bethlehem. He knew that his victory over mankind was threatened. From Herod's laughter of the innocent babies to the cross, satan tried to derail Jesus' mission. Yet Jesus never wavered and He never sinned. He taught. He served. He spoke. He listened. He walked toward His destiny with the peace of purpose that comes when we walk in the center of God's will. Jesus said **He** laid down His life. He showed me that there is always a choice. I believe that is the ultimate piece that makes the sacrifice perfect—**choosing** to do it. It was not the nails that held Jesus to the cross. I t was His love for me – for you.

> *But God commends his own love toward us, in that while we were yet sinners, Christ died for us.*
>
> Romans 5:8 (WEB)

The suffering of Christ was not in the scourging and the cross. Men before Him and after have experienced such a death. It was the spiritual suffering of taking the **total** sins of all mankind. He who was sinless – became sin – losing all sense of the Father's presence that He had always known. In that hour – alone – "My God, why have **You** forsaken me?" There is no way for me to know, comprehend, the value of that sacrifice. Jesus did not need that sacrifice for Himself. He only did it for me. He only did it for you.

Only in the cross can sin be atoned. Only in the cross can there be **forgiveness** for my sin. Only in the cross can I **begin** to see God's extravagant love. Only in the cross is there salvation, **eternal life**.

Pay Attention   September 15

> *Command and teach these things. Let no man despise your youth; but* be an example *to those who believe, in word, in your way of life, in love, in spirit, in faith, and in purity. Until I come, pay attention to reading, to exhortation, and to teaching.* Don't neglect *the gift that is in you, which was given to you by prophecy, with the laying on of the hands of the elders.* Be diligent *in these things. Give yourself* **wholly** *to them, that your progress may be revealed to all.* Pay attention *to yourself, and to your teaching.* Continue *in these things, for in doing this you will save both yourself and those who hear you.*
>
> 1 Timothy 4:11-16 (WEB, *my emphasis*)

I hope you will take the time to read this Scripture again. If the translation here is a bit too unfamiliar, pull out your Bible and read it **slowly** and let it simmer in your spirit.

This is a passage that I have not read many times. I would say that I have read it only when I was encouraging a youth in their call. Paul told Timothy that **all** Scripture is useful. (2 Timothy 3:16) Silly me not to have got the **all** part! This Scripture is for me also.

I may not be considered "youth" but God's words are also pointed to me. "Let no one despise your gender, Jody, or your age." Nothing is an excuse (or prejudice) that keeps me from **being an example** in **all** facets of my life. The excuses of others can only impact the ministry that God has called me if I **let** them! Is there any aspect of my life not covered in the words "love, spirit, faith, purity"? I can't think of one.

Then there is the strong admonition to "pay attention". Most of us have a teacher (or two or three) that has sharply spoken those words! What has my attention? What I read? What I am taught? And what strongly urges or warns me? I believe that means I am not only to "pay attention" as in understand and take in but also be careful what has my attention. Test the spirits, remember?

"Be diligent" and "do not neglect" the gifts and opportunities that God has given me. If I waste His time and talents, He will withdraw them and give them to someone who will pay attention! I should be **growing** in my ministry. There should be progress. God does not expect me to stay in kindergarten and He surely will not put up with my crazy teen years in ministry! David Ravenhill wrote a wonderful book, *For God's Sake, Grow Up!* (ISBN#1560432993) on that very subject.

A warning is clear to me: Have some **Holy Fear** about what you teach. Whatever is taught to me must go through God's sifting and pass **His** test first and **then** I pass it along to someone else. I am responsible for what I teach. It's power (or lack) may have eternal consequences in another life. Holy Fear...give that some thought today along with careless words. My witness to Jesus in my life.

Is that You, God?   September 16

Give ear to my words, Yahweh. Consider my meditation. Listen to the voice of my cry, my King and my God; for to you do I pray. Yahweh, in the morning you shall hear my voice. In the morning I will lay my requests before you, and will watch expectantly.

Psalm 5:1-3 (WEB)

I think the most frequently asked questions I get when teaching about prayer and an intimate relationship with God are, "How do I know it is God talking to me?" and "How do I know that I am following the will of God?" Good questions. I don't think the answers are difficult but their application is contrary to my nature!

God is truthful. His words today do not negate His words of 2000 years ago. So when I believe I hear His voice, what He is saying to me will line up with what He said to Paul two centuries ago. God will not tell me that it is OK for me to worry about my children. He will not tell me that what I am dealing with now is more difficult than anything Paul had to do -- so my worry is justified. No, God is able to take care of my concerns just like He did Paul's.

I believe that I know I am **in** the will of God because that place has a very distinctive characteristic: peace. The will of God may be a place that is outside my 'nature' or my 'flesh' but my spirit recognizes it and it is a place of peace for my spirit. My family and I have been through difficult 'seasons' including a time when my youngest son had a recurrent cancer. Through

127

every step as we decided about doctors, place of treatment, path of treatment, and timing, God directed each step. The difficult task was to 'wait' on Him. We might have a question at 8 a.m. on Tuesday morning and the clear answer did not show itself until Thursday at noon. When it came, it was clear and it came with such peace! Waiting was difficult! I wanted the answer on Tuesday at 8:05 a.m.!!! But waiting brought the perfect answer and the perfect peace!!!

Blessed are the poor in spirit, for theirs is the Kingdom of Heaven.

Blessed are those who mourn, for they shall be comforted.
Blessed are the gentle, for they shall inherit the earth.
Blessed are those who hunger and thirst after righteousness, for they shall be filled.
Blessed are the merciful, for they shall obtain mercy.
Blessed are the pure in heart, for they shall see God.
Blessed are the peacemakers, for they shall be called children of God.
Blessed are those who have been persecuted for righteousness' sake,
for theirs is the Kingdom of Heaven...
But seek first God's Kingdom, and his righteousness; and all these things will be given to you as well
Matthew 5:3-10, 6:33 (WEB)

If you haven't read Matthew 5 and 6 in the last 3 months, I encourage you to take time this week and do so. There is so much in those two chapters that I think that I could read it every day for a month and still get something new every time! Jesus' words during the Sermon on the Mount are often quoted in discussions about God's will and obedience until the words seem almost cliché. They are **not** cliché. They are succinct and true! The tough part about hearing from God and **knowing** that I am hearing Him is the building of my relationship with God by following Jesus' example. Seeking **first** God's kingdom and a right relationship with Him and **then** put everything else in a list below that! This doesn't happen over night. It comes with a growing, living relationship with my Lord.

God, My Teacher   September 17

Husbands, love your wives, even as Christ also loved the assembly, and gave himself up for it; that he might sanctify it, having cleansed it by the washing of water with the word, that he might present the assembly to himself gloriously, not having spot or wrinkle or any such thing; but that it should be holy and without blemish. Even so husbands also ought to love their own wives as their own bodies. He who loves his own wife loves himself. For no man ever hated his own flesh; but nourishes and cherishes it, even as the Lord also does the assembly; because we are members of his body, of his flesh and bones. "For this cause a man will leave his father and mother, and will be joined to his wife. The two will become one flesh." [Genesis 2:24] This mystery is great, but I speak concerning Christ and of the assembly. Nevertheless each of you must also love his own wife even as himself; and let the wife see that she respects her husband.

Ephesians 5:25-33 (WEB)

I am looking at Scriptures this week that I may not have thought applied to me but since all Scripture is good for teaching (2 Timothy 3:16), I have reconsidered!

This is one of many Scriptures that would have been good to commit to memory as a young girl. It give the characteristics of a God-loving, God-fearing man.

The man who loves God first is one with his priorities at a good beginning. I knew my husband, Henry, loved God before I knew anything else except his name. I knew his testimony before I knew about his family or his income. His humility and kindness made his looks just an added bonus!

129

The man who considers his wife's needs first may not always remember you like waffles over pancakes but he is going to know and remember what God has gifted you to do in ministry. That fact will weigh on the decisions for where you worship; even where you live. There was a time when a ministry opportunity for me appeared to be opening. It would have meant a move. Henry was willing to move. Henry wants me to fulfill my call.

Leaving your parents and joining with your spouse is more than geography and sex. It is a covenant, a holy vow and commitment, between you, your spouse, and God. No one – **no one** - gets another place at that table. Not your parents. Not your children.

Your spouse should know without a doubt that he/she is #2 in your life after God. You do not sacrifice your spouse in order to please your parents. Your decisions should reflect the characteristics of you and your spouse as a unit -- not those of your parents. Your children should know that "Mom and Dad time" is important and worthy of consideration and respect. They should know that Mom and Dad love each other and so their home is a place of love, respect, and forgiveness. Children should know how to say, "I'm sorry" because they have heard their parents say it to each other -- and to them.

Marriage is passion that goes far beyond the physical. It is love sifted through your relationship with God that brings more compassion, kindness, gentleness joy, faith, peace, patience, and, yes, self-control and mercy (forgiveness) than you ever thought possible to give -- and receive. It is a mystery - a miracle.

Now when he [Jesus] saw the crowds, he went up on a mountainside and sat down. His disciples came to him, and he began to teach them,...

Matthew 5:1-2 (NIV)

I am blessed with a husband who leads by example. (Relax, Henry. I am not going to embarrass you by implying that you are perfect!) His devotionals reflect his relationship with God. He **listens** to God. It **is** so important to learn; to sit at Jesus' feet and **listen**!

Jesus went up on the mountain. He found a spot good for listening and good for speaking. I understand from some friends who have visited that mountain in Galilee that the acoustics are **perfect**!

Jesus went up on the mountain and **sat down**. He was in no hurry. He had something to say. It was important. In the Jewish culture, when the rabbi was going to teach, he sat down. Did you ever notice that when the Pope speaks, he sits down? Jesus had a hungry audience. Jesus had a divine appointment!

Jesus was not just there to teach "the crowds". He also had disciples to teach. Maybe they were the primary target.

I attended a Bible study in the last year on the book of Romans. While reading *God's Generals II* by Roberts Liardon, I had discovered that Martin Luther went from passive priest to passionate reformer after studying Romans. So when I discovered my pastor's new Bible study was Romans, I felt my spirit leap and knew I also had a divine appointment. I have searched for many months for a study to which God was inviting me. Great things are worth the time to search. God's words – His teaching – are of great price!

Your word is a lamp to my feet and light for my path.

Psalm 119:105 (NIV)

Get in a Bible study this fall. Listen! Learn! Be challenged! Soak up God's words for you like a sponge! This is a 'God-way' for you to be **squeezed out** on a thirsty world!

Words of Life II   September 19

Remind them to be in subjection to rulers and to authorities, to be obedient, to be ready *for every good work, to speak evil of no one, not to be contentious,* to be gentle, *showing all humility toward all men. For we were also once foolish, disobedient, deceived, serving various lusts and pleasures, living in malice and envy, hateful, and hating one another. But* when the kindness of God *our Savior and his love toward mankind appeared, not by works of righteousness, which we did ourselves,* but according to his mercy, he saved us, *through the washing of regeneration and renewing by the Holy Spirit, whom he poured out on us* richly, *through Jesus Christ our Savior; that, being justified by his grace, we might be made heirs according to the hope of eternal life. This saying is faithful, and concerning these things I desire that you affirm confidently, so that* those who have believed God may be careful to maintain good works. *These things are good and* profitable *to men; but shun foolish questionings, genealogies, strife, and disputes about the law; for they are unprofitable and vain. Avoid a factious man after a first and second warning; knowing that such a one is perverted, and sins, being self-condemned.*

                                        Titus 3:1-11 (WEB)

This has been a **profitable** week for me. I have learned a lot in verses that I do not read (even avoid!). God is so very faithful and patient to nudge (or drag) me in the path that He desires so He can bless me.

This passage begins by telling me to "be obedient" and I believe it is in that obedience that I **am** ready for whatever good work He has in mind for me. And then I hear so quietly but firmly what are the facets of character that God desires to develop in me. He wants my mouth to bring forth only good, not evil. "Contentious" is argumentative. It is the characteristic of someone who wants to be recognized as **right**! Was Jesus seen as always right? Did it matter to Him? Did Jesus argue the Pharisees or Pilate down? Jesus was gentle and humble and yet seen as strong and spoke with authority. He shows me how to allow my strength and authority to come from God. If I am "right" in the Father's eyes, the opinion of anyone else is – just a frill.

The power and joy that comes through the words that remind me that it was the **kindness** of God that saved me. It was **nothing** that I deserved but just the **mercy** the came from God's extraordinary love that **continues** to pour out even today! It is a spring of eternal life that is there whether I see my day as joyous or full of trials. The question is do I try to put up my own umbrella and shield myself for what I believe is beating down on me or do I just stand there (like a child) with my arms outstretched knowing that my Father will pour out **His** abundance on His child.

And finally I read the wise words that tell me to keep my eyes on Jesus, following His footsteps in the good work of the day; turning away from whatever is not Kingdom building. Remember how God stripped Peter and Paul away from the Pharisee-thinking that was clinging to them about what was proper to eat, circumcision or not circumcision, and so many of laws that tangled them. As a modern man of God has said, "Quit majoring on the minors!" Whatever causes factions – is not God!

I hope you will join us and spend time in God's word. Allow it to simmer on the burner of your spirit, cooking down, developing rich, intense flavor that is nourishment and life.

Even though I am working this weekend I am going to keep His word close by and sip those words of life. I do not want to get dehydrated!

No "Lone Rangers"   September 20

"You are the salt of the earth, but if the salt has lost its flavor, with what will it be salted? It is then good for nothing, but to be cast out and trodden under the feet of men."

Matthew 5:13 (WEB)

Be sober and self-controlled. Be watchful. Your adversary, the devil, walks around like a roaring lion, seeking whom he may devour. Withstand him steadfast in your faith, knowing that your brothers who are in the world are undergoing the same sufferings.

1 Peter 5:8-9 (WEB)

Here are two Scriptures that speak to me and answer why I should be surrounded, connected, to the Body of Believers.

Peter warns that our enemy, satan, never rests from looking for an opportunity to ambush a believer. Satan knows that his time is short and he wants to cause as much damage and death as he can. He goes for the easy target. Who is an easy target? The one who believes he is OK listening to a preacher on TV and has only "me, myself, and I" as a study partner? Or the one who worships and studies with others and so has a network of prayer partners and 'family' who seeks god's will together? Satan would rather fight **one** than an **army**! Sobriety and self-control has proven to flourish when those of like minds come together to witness and encourage each other. The same group watches out for each other, waving a red flag when danger approaches.

Jesus said we are salt. Salt is flavor and it is a preserver. As I was discussing the Matthew passage with my husband, he pointed out that Jesus may have been encouraging His small group of disciples that a little salt provides a big flavor and so they, though small, will bring great impact. In the Body of Believers (for good – or not) we each impact the Body and the Kingdom. We are to provide good 'flavor' in our walk, allowing the Father to use us where and to whom He will. We can become 'flat' and of no use if we do not stay connected and filled.

The problems in the established church are many. I refuse to give in to obvious opportunities to bash but instead ask God to correct in me and share what He teaches me as He sees fit. The Body of Believers where I am connected is not primarily inside a building called a church. It is a network of brothers and sisters across the world of many backgrounds. We all love the Lord and are seeking Jesus' direction in every aspect of our lives. We share and study and pray with each other and for each other. I am blessed to know that this close group will not only lift me up but love me enough to honestly speak words of love, even to discipline. I need encouragement and discipline!

See how good and how pleasant it is for brothers [and sisters!] *to live together in unity!*
It is like the precious oil on the head, that ran down on the beard,
even Aaron's beard; that came down on the edge of his robes;
like the dew of Hermon, that comes down on the hills of Zion:
for there Yahweh gives the blessing, even life forevermore.
                                        Psalm 133 (WEB, my addition)

LIVE FREE!   September 21

In those days, John the Baptizer came, preaching in the wilderness of Judea, saying, "Repent, for the Kingdom of Heaven is at hand!"

                                        Matthew 3:1-2 (WEB)

Do I know what it means to repent? Turn away from sin. Walk in God's path.

Do I live like I have repented? John said, that the kingdom of God was **near**. He was speaking of a kingdom where God would rule and reign. A kingdom where God would **live with us**! If I have repented of my sins – am I not living **with God**? Is He not in my heart? Isn't my spirit is in relationship with His Spirit?

The disciples did not live their lives free from hardship and disease. The Bible and history tell us that all died a martyr's death except John and I wonder if his death may have been the most difficult of all!

Paul speaks of Timothy's "frequent illnesses" (1 Timothy 5) and his own torment of the "thorn" which could have been a physical or spiritual ailment. In any case, the life of a Believer will have sickness and seasons of great trials, even suffering. Does that mean our faith is weak?

God is all about kingdom building. He wants – even desires that **all** would come to know Him. There is nothing like cancer or death – a crisis – to get an unbeliever's attention and consider that they just may not have everything under their control as they thought!

God may be **allowing** a crisis in **my** life so that His Light – His Presence in this repented heart can shine in a dark world that is **desperate** for a **true Light**! Not some glossed-over, self-help way but a **true** walk that is full of **God's courage** and **God's peace** in the middle of a storm.

When you think God is not answering your prayer for healing – look up! Your victory is already there! **The Kingdom of God is near!**

"Comfort, comfort my people," says your God. "Speak comfortably to Jerusalem; and call out to her that her warfare is accomplished, that her iniquity is pardoned, that she has received of Yahweh's hand double for all her sins."
The voice of one who calls out,
"Prepare the way of Yahweh in the wilderness! Make a level highway in the desert for our God.
Every valley shall be exalted, and every mountain and hill shall be made low.
The uneven shall be made level, and the rough places a plain.
The glory of Yahweh shall be
revealed, and all flesh shall see it together; for the mouth of Yahweh has spoken it."
The voice of one saying, "Cry!"
One said, "What shall I cry?"
"All flesh is like grass, and all its glory is like the flower of the field. The grass withers, the flower fades, because Yahweh's breath blows on it. Surely the people are like grass. The grass withers, the flower fades; but the word of our God stands forever."

Isaiah 40:1-8 (WEB)

God's chosen people spent many generations wandering in a desert or exiled or fighting enemies and then taken prisoner and exiled again! They grieved for their loss of home; their relationship with Yahweh.

I grieve today. Compared to Israel my loss is very new, very personal, and even small by Kingdom size. My Father, my compassionate, loving Father does not compare my grief. He just sees His child's heart hurting and pours out His comfort. His comfort is personal and extravagant, lavish as it comes perfectly to the spot that aches and weeps.

His comfort does not just come as a balm but it also brings hope. It brings the promise that the valley will be made level. If my steps today seem to be on a rocky stretch, God promises He will clear the way and offers His hand to steady my stumbling steps even before I know I need the help.

God's comfort does not minimize my grief as foolish but validates that this life is fleeting and when death comes there is sorrow at the separation. He gently reminds me that the separation will be but a season as He has promised that we who put our trust in Him will be reunited with Him and each other for **all** eternity. The mouth of God has spoken and I can put my trust in Him.

And so today I am separated and saddened by that separation. But I have this Hope that promises what I now cannot see but believe by faith and I have the testimonies of the very ones who have gone before me.

Repentance Part I   September 23

Now after John was taken into custody, Jesus came into Galilee, preaching the Good News of the Kingdom of God, and saying, "The time is fulfilled, and the Kingdom of God is at hand! Repent, and believe in the Good News."

Mark 1:14-15 (WEB)

In my studies I have noticed that God is all about three's. Repentance is in all three levels of my being.

It is my mind. I acknowledge my sin. Every day, I get quiet and let God through His Holy Spirit turn the flashlight on my life. I picture in my mind how He looks under my bed where I don't clean very often, in the closet of my life where I think I have locked the ugliness away, and in that forgotten corner where the cobwebs cling. "Create in me a clean heart, God." (Psalm 51 is a good thing to pray during this time.)

It is my emotions. If I can scream and shout at a baseball game, but neither my sin that separates me from my Creator nor the moment when I realize that I am forgiven produce a tear – then I may need a emotion priority check! Have you ever choked up during a sermon or while reading a passage of Scripture? That's God touching you! He is coming close and you are aware of the gulf between you – and He bridged the gap with Jesus! **That's emotional!**

It is my will. There is the center of truth in repentance. I make a determined choice to turn from sin, change my attitude about the sin and about God, and purpose to avoid the temptation of that sin.

> *No temptation has taken you except what is common to man. God is faithful, who will not allow you to be tempted above what you are able, but will with the temptation also make the way of escape, that you may be able to endure it.*
>
> 1 Corinthians 10:13 (WEB)

Only God's power through His Spirit can give me the resolve to be truly repentant and walk as a **new** person each day! Our churches are filled with people who go to church when it is convenient to their activity schedule, give their money and support church activities, and even compliment the pastor on his sermon. Talking the language of a Christian does not reflect the repentant heart. A repented heart is one that is surrendered to God and shows in everything that we do!

The God Place   September 24

> *Six days later Jesus took Peter and James and John and brought them to a high mountain apart from the rest, and his appearance was changed in front of them. And his clothes became sparkling white, much whiter than any bleach on earth could make them. And Elijah appeared to them with Moses, and the two of them*

were talking with Jesus. And Peter responded by saying to Jesus, "Rabbi! This is a good place to be! Let's make three shelters, one for you, one for Moses, and one for Elijah." He said this because he didn't know what he was saying, because they were terrified. Then a cloud overshadowed them, and there was a voice that came from the cloud: "This is my beloved son, listen to him!" And immediately after that they didn't see anything, except Jesus himself with them.

Mark 9:2-8 (HN)

I hope that we have all had experiences when Jesus was especially close to us and at the same time when he was especially glorious. Those are the high points that can help us through our Christian journey.

I don't know where your high points are, or how you experience them. For some people it's a time of worship in music. For me it has most commonly been when I have taken on a passage of scripture to study thoroughly. I pray, read the passage many times, ask myself questions about it and meditate on the answers. There will be times when I feel Jesus right there telling me about that passage. For others, it may be a time of retreat.

Whatever it is, if you have experienced it, you'll be in some sympathy with Peter here. The one thing that you know is that you really want to stay right there and never move. It's too precious a moment and too wonderful a feeling. I have a friend who will say that there are no drugs that can create a high as good as God's presence. (To those of you who might worry, let me assure you that my friend is not saying that the presence of God is like a drug high, only better. What he's saying is that God's presence is so there - that you have no hope of counterfeiting it with drugs.)

You really want to set up camp. You really want to stay there. But hear me: This is only a taste! The disciples are just tasting God's presence. They are just tasting being with Jesus in his glory. That overwhelming experience is not the real thing. That's why you can't set up camp as Peter wanted to. It's not that this is bad; it's just that this is not where you're really going.

Here's some things we can learn about spiritual experience from this passage:

– It's something God gives us to keep us going.

– We can't camp where it happens. God's kingdom is inside (Luke 17:21). God can visit you wherever you are!

– It won't answer all your questions. The disciples had to go on discussing the resurrection.

– It's just a taste. The full glory comes when we see Jesus face to face.

Let's not just look for the experience, but let the experience of God's presence empower us for the next step! Let's find the good place that goes with us all the time.

Repentance: Part II   September 25

He [Jesus] called the multitude to himself with his disciples, and said to them, "Whoever wants to come after me, let him deny himself, and take up his cross, and follow me. For whoever wants to save his life will lose it; and whoever will lose his life for my sake and the sake of the Good News will save it. For what does it profit a man, to gain the whole world, and forfeit his life? For what will a man give in exchange for his life? For whoever will be ashamed of me and of my words in this adulterous and sinful generation, the Son of Man also will be ashamed of him, when he comes in the glory of his Father with the holy angels."

Mark 8:34-38 (WEB)

'Surrender' is the part of repentance that even after 15 years of never-turning-back commitment to Jesus – I still struggle. To

141

surrender means I relinquish control. What does that mean in context of a relationship with God?

God spoke all these words, saying, "I am Yahweh your God, who brought you out of the land of Egypt, out of the house of bondage.

"You shall have no other gods before me."

Exodus 20:1-3 (WEB)

God says it is His way and only His way. That may sound harsh but do we not say that to our own children as we are walking in a crowded mall or busy street? God is a good Father. His desire is that we live with Him, whole and healthy. When we choose to walk away from Him, we **will** live unwisely. Jesus gave us the beautiful parable of the Prodigal Son. (Luke 15) The son chooses his own way. He finds the error in this and calls it **sin**. He feels he is "not worthy" to come home to the Father. He finds the Father waiting with arms open. The son had only to turn to the Father and say, "I'm sorry for doing it my way" and "Yes" to the Father's plan for his life.

Choosing to live my life on God's plan means talking to Him about my dreams and hopes. It is also listening to Him about what opportunities He is opening for me. It is a day-to-day relationship that grows because it is **alive!**

God is faithful to show His love for me. I see Him opening doors and inspiring me with what I need to function in these new opportunities. Let me give a short, persona l example/testimony:

When Henry and I knew it was time for me to go back to work, God opened the door to two places I would never have chosen. I have worked in places that some would say I was overqualified to work. I was not sent there to impress anyone with my great nursing gifts. I was sent to those jobs to minister and sow God's seeds into people I would not have met in my daily life. I have earned a living, prayed with people, and surrendered my plan for God's plan.

> All to Jesus I surrender,
> All to Him I freely give;
> I will ever love and trust Him,
> In his presence daily live.
> I surrender all, I surrender all;
> All to thee, my blessed Savior, I surrender all.
>
> All to Jesus I surrender,
> Humbly at His feet I bow,
> Worldly pleasures all forsaken,
> Take me Jesus, take me now.
> I surrender all, I surrender all;
> All to thee, my blessed Savior, I surrender all.

Words by Judson W. Van DeVenter,

Music by Winfield S. Weeden, 1896

For What are You Hoping? September 26

Now faith is the substantial nature of things we hope for, the clear conviction of things we don't see. By this means the elders were approved.
By faith we understand that the universe was made by the word of God, so that things which are seen didn't come out of things already visible...

Therefore restore the weakened hands and the bent knees, and prepare straight paths for your feet so that the lame might not stumble but rather might be healed.

-- Hebrews 11:1-3; 12:12-13 (HN)

As I was reading this passage, my attention was repeatedly drawn to the word "hope." I have never really talked that much about hope before. I'm pretty much a "facts" person. I like to

143

be realistic. Even when I'm going out on a limb, I like to remind myself regularly how far out I am, how thin that limb is getting, and how close to the ground it's bending.

You could say that I walk by faith, but with a powerful emphasis on how hard it is. I take the step of faith, while making sure I'm clear that I'm really stepping over the edge.

When I was slowly walking away from the church after seminary, many people told me that all I needed to do was have faith. The problem was, you might say, that the lack of faith was precisely the problem. Not one person suggested that I look for hope. I wonder why that is. Since then I've heard many, many sermons on faith for every sermon on hope I've heard. Yet in the classic verse we use for defending our faith, we're told to be prepared to give a reason for our hope.

Now look at our text for today. In Hebrews 12:12-13 we are told to strengthen those who are weak. Do you suppose we do this by telling them how they ought to be strong, or is there something else we need to do? Then move back to Hebrews 11:1-3. Faith is the "substantial nature," the real essence of the things that we hope for. Faith connects us to our hope!

But what if we try to have faith without hope? Well, our faith may move us forward, but we will certainly miss the joy, and we may lose the faith. Some of us seem to adhere to a John Wayne theory of faith - if we're just tough enough, we'll succeed. But God knows we need hope.

For what are you hoping today?

Eternal Anchor of Hope   September 27

If Christ has not been raised, your faith is vain; you are still in your sins. [18]Then they also who are fallen asleep in Christ have perished. [19]If we have only hoped in Christ in this life, we are of all men most pitiable.

1 Corinthians 15:17-19 (WEB)

This hope we have as an anchor of the soul, a hope both sure and steadfast...

Hebrews 6:19 (WEB)

Hope must have its origin in Jesus. If I do not believe that Jesus died, rose from dead, and now lives eternally, then my hope for **anything** is certainly built on a foundation of sand.

I have many hopes in and for my life, as long as it lasts here on this earth. I **hope** to be able to spend more time with my grandchildren over the next ten years than I have the last ten years. I **hope** to be able to have more opportunities to encourage and teach others how to grow into mature disciples. I **hope** God will allow Henry and me to network with more Christians who do not know each other now but will come together to build His Kingdom.

These hopes are alive because I **know** the assurance of the Hope of eternal life. Jesus is so real and His love so tangible that the gift of eternal life was given freely and I took it into my heart with that same freedom. With tiny, faltering, baby steps of faith, I was given Hope big enough to support all my other hopes and, yes, dreams. Jesus' Hope is the anchor that keeps my life from being battered beyond repair in the storms of this life. I have been through some hurricanes! (And not just physical ones!) In those dark and uncertain moments, it is the anchor of Jesus' hope that brings my eyes up to His eyes and I am no longer flailing among the high waves but, in fact, walking with Him on the water. Like Peter, the walk occurs when I go forth with a tiny drop of faith, no strength of my own, and know only that Jesus is the only way; that there is no other option. I **will not** abandon my walk with Him no matter how many times I stumble. Jesus is my anchor. [Read Peter's experiences: Matthew 14:22-33, John 5:66-69]

He doesn't delight in the strength of the horse. He takes no pleasure in the legs of a man.
Yahweh takes pleasure in those who fear him, in those who hope in his loving kindness.

Psalm 147:10-11 (WEB)

Why are you in despair, my soul? Why are you disturbed within me?
Hope in God! For I shall still praise him for the saving help of his presence.

Psalm 42:5 (WEB)

It is so simple and yet so hard for me to stop struggling to make something happen; pushing to move the boulder in my path and instead take Jesus' hand and rest in His timing and care. It is not for me to just sit but instead to seek Jesus and His plan, keeping myself fit and ready. It is living in the peace that surrounds my Hope in Jesus, firm and secure in His forever love.

My Salty Self   September 28

[Jesus said] *"Salt is good, but if the salt has lost its saltiness, with what will you season it? Have salt in yourselves, and be at peace with one another."*

Mark 9:50 (WEB)

My pastor preached about being salty one Sunday. The title was "Have Salt in Yourself". I came away considering the Church. Why do we avoid being salty?

Just think about foods that we eat every day and consider how they would taste without salt. Eggs. Tomatoes. French fries. Some foods like olives and pickles would not even exist without salt. Without salt in these foods, they would be defined as bland. Most of us are not attracted to bland food. How many are attracted to bland Church? When you think of Jesus and His words and ministry, does the word **bland** come to mind? No, not for me either.

> [LORD said,] *"Every offering of your meal offering you shall season with salt; neither shall you allow the salt of the covenant of your God to be lacking from your meal offering. With all your offerings you shall offer salt."*
>
> *Leviticus 2:13 (WEB)*

Do you think Jesus was remembering His words to the Israelites when He spoke about saltiness several centuries later to His then disciples? When He speaks to me about saltiness? I think He is still trying to get His message across. We keep trying to water down His messages, making them bland and tasteless. We want to "fit in" and be "politically correct" more than we want to be 'salty' as Jesus exhorted us to be.

I am called by Jesus to bring **flavor** into the world. That **flavor** is to have characteristics like salt:

– good flavor, not bitter or sour
– balanced, putting the amount in that Jesus directs making the end product palatable, not bland but not too much which can produce nausea
– preserving that which is good
– of value; of worth. Salt was currency. What God wants me to give is not cheap but it is free.

The ministry of these devotions would be considered the **saltiness** that God has given to me to give away. Though I may see myself as only the scribe to His inspiring words, it is my choice to make the commitment to the ministry and to obediently write without tainting the salt of His words. (salt vs. garlic salt) God's words may not always be what I **want** to hear but they are always what I **need** to hear. This is what we should

147

be hearing and speaking to each other. Church is a place of **saltiness**. One of the ways I am replenished. It is a matter worthy of daily prayer.

Who is Jesus?   September 29

(This is my homework for the weekly Bible study that I am attending.)

Now when Jesus came into the parts of Caesarea Philippi, he asked his disciples, saying, "Who do men say that I, the Son of Man, am?"...
Simon Peter answered, "You are the Christ, the Son of the living God."

Matthew 16:13, 16 (WEB)

Who is Jesus? As a believing Christian with 2000 years of Hindsight the answer seems like a no-brainer: He is the Messiah. Peter's answer comes without the hindsight. It comes **from** his heart by the power of God. I know that because Jesus said so.

What is **my** heart answer to the question: Who is Jesus?

Jesus is my look into my Father. He says He and the Father are one. (John 10:30) When I read Jesus' words, see what He does, and feel His compassion and love, (and discipline!) I am able to know the Father more. Jesus atoned for my sins and so bridged the gap between my sinfulness and God's holiness. Jesus continues to bring the Father and me together.

Jesus is also the best friend and love that I have. He is always there. 24/7. He always has His ears tuned to my voice. He always knows when I need Him and for what I need Him. He is never too busy or distracted by "stuff". I am **never** alone. Jesus is the Alpha and Omega. (Revelation 22:13)

Finally, Jesus is the Messiah; the son of the living God. I am a simple, pragmatic woman so the first two **bring me** to the third. In this difficult, suffering world, it is the third that brings me hope for each day. Jesus is **living** and active in my life. It is a daily relationship that grows and, hopefully, matures. He is the Savior.

My soul, wait in silence for God alone, for my expectation is from him.
He alone is my rock and my salvation, my fortress. I will not be shaken.
With God is my salvation and my honor. The rock of my strength, and my refuge, is in God.
Trust in him at all times, you people. Pour out your heart before him. God is a refuge for us.

Psalm 62:5-8 (WEB)

Jesus... I am listening!   September 30

They went out from there, and passed through Galilee. He didn't want anyone to know it. For he was teaching his disciples, and said to them, "The Son of Man is being handed over to the hands of men, and they will kill him; and when he is killed, on the third day he will rise again."
But they didn't understand the saying, and were afraid to ask him.

Mark 9:30-32 (WEB)

One of the questions I ask myself every time I write a devotion: "Is what You are saying to me, Lord, **only** for me or am I to pass this along?" Most days not **everything** is to be passed along. God is so—**perfectly God**—to be able to take His words and focus them through the power of His Spirit **exactly** into my heart. And I know He does this for many of you because you testify with your comments and emails and I rejoice when it is a little "nugget" that God delivers just for you!

Jesus did not give all teaching to everyone. In reading the

gospels, we are told that only Peter, James, and John accompanied Jesus to the moment of transfiguration, the raising of dead girl, and His most intimate time in the Garden. Here in this passage of Mark, Jesus is bringing His disciples to a time apart from the usual crowds to give them an important piece of prophecy. He tells them openly (and clearly) that He is going to die and will rise on the third day. Why wouldn't they understand those words? Because it was not what they wanted to hear.

Jesus speaks to me like that, too. He speaks a truth to me. I say "I don't understand" or I pretend it is not for **me** but "**surely** for that one over there"! If I cannot be **nakedly honest** with Jesus, then with who? Jesus is leading me down the path to growing, to healing, to learning which produces a closer relationship.

The disciples fear the truths and so they believe that if they do not ask, Jesus will not tell! If I don't ask Jesus who **knows** the answers then who **will** I be trusting? Truth can be scary but truth from Jesus comes with the assurance of the One who speaks. Some would say that "Jesus doesn't give you more than you can handle". I actually think that I have received much more than I can handle on my own! When I **allow** Jesus to carry the most weight, I can walk through some difficult truths and hear His voice explain and speak to my heart. It is a relationship with dialogue. We discuss what He is saying. It is a wonderful, intimate experience.

There is no question that I cannot ask Jesus. I can ask the question and know that He will hear it better than I can say it and answer it better than I can imagine. We have 'discussed' here before how I need to be open to Jesus' answer which may be outside of my expectation. The answer will always line up with proven characteristics of Jesus but it may stretch **my** plan. Jesus truly has the Big Picture and so my life **must** be flexible enough to move in the opportunities that open to be a **tool** in

His Hands. WOW!

Let's take time to ask Jesus to give us the courage to hear what He wants to say today. Gives us ears to hear and hearts to receive, Jesus, in Your name we pray. Amen.

Soup Kitchen for the Soul

What I Didn't Learn in Church,

I Learned in a Soup Kitchen!

$12.99

Soup Kitchen for the Soul combines testimony with a challenging scriptural foundation and follows it with specific guidance on how you can get out of your church and make a difference in your community. Each chapter builds on a Bible story and the author's personal experience, and ends with thought questions, and then action questions. References include specific ways in which you can take action on what you have been studying in the book.

This book is suitable for personal or small group study, or could be used effectively by an entire church to transform their ministry.

In the introduction Crosby says: "Upon entering Seminary, I was required to serve in the community and begrudgingly accepted my assignment, choosing to serve in a soup kitchen. While serving in the soup kitchen, God revealed himself to me in a profound and miraculous way. It was in restudying the scriptures with this new heart knowledge of God that allowed me to see a message of a mission for His people that we lack a connection with today. I began asking, 'What if ... What if I'm not the only one who doesn't understand the whole mission God has planned for us? What exactly are we supposed to be doing? Where in the Bible can we find directives on our missions for God? What if I wrote a book about radically new old ways of doing the gospel?'"

Soup Kitchen for the Soul is that book.

Coming August 1, 2010

Along Bible Paths: Autumn Devotions

If you've enjoyed these devotionals, then keep your eye open for fall devotions. Henry and Jody Neufeld again combine to provide a quarter of daily devotionals for autumn.

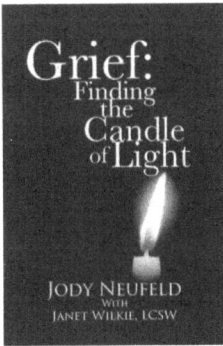

Grief: Finding the Candle of Light

Jody Neufeld talks about facing grief as a Christian, speaking from personal experience and scripture.

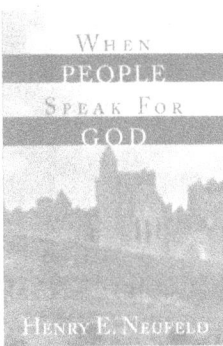

When People Speak for God

Henry Neufeld discusses how we can discern the voice of God, combining an understanding of personal experience with God, the gift of prophecy and Biblical inspiration.

Available
via
Energion Direct
energiondirect.com
or at other major online retailers.

More from Energion Publications

Personal Study

The Jesus Paradigm	$17.99
When People Speak for God	$17.99
The Character of Our Discontent	$12.99
Holy Smoke, Unholy Fire	$14.99
Not Ashamed of the Gospel	$12.99
Evidence for the Bible	$16.99
Christianity and Secularism	$16.99
What's In A Version?	$12.99
Christian Archy	$9.99
The Messiah and His Kingdom to Come	$19.99 (B&W)
(an EnerPower Press title)	$49.99 (Color)

Christian Living

52 Weeks of Ordinary People – Extraordinary God	$7.99
Daily Devotions of Ordinary People – Extraordinary God	$19.99
Directed Paths	$7.99
Grief: Finding the Candle of Light	$8.99
I Want to Pray	$7.99
Soup Kitchen for the Soul	$12.99

Bible Study for Groups

Learning and Living Scripture	$12.99
To the Hebrews: A Participatory Study Guide	$9.99
Revelation: A Participatory Study Guide	$9.99
The Gospel According to St. Luke: A Participatory Study Guide	$8.99
Identifying Your Gifts and Service: Small Group Edition	$12.99
Consider Christianity, Volume I & II Study Guides	$7.99 each

Politics

Preserving Democracy (Hardcover)	$29.99

Fiction

Tales from Jevlir: Oddballs	$7.99
(an Enzar Empire Press title)	
Megabelt	$12.99

Generous Quantity Discounts Available
Dealer Inquiries Welcome

Energion Publications

P.O. Box 841

Gonzalez, FL 32560

Website: http://energionpubs.com
Phone: (850) 525-3916